cities full of space
qualities of density

cities full of space
qualities of density

rudy uytenhaak

010 publishers rotterdam

cities full of space
qualities of density

a city should bustle

I've called my story Cities Full of Space. For cities are not merely the museums and theatres of everyday life, in which we experience what occupies people in the broad scope of their lives, they are also ingenious spatial constellations that bring together people and their activities – in all their diversity: from dynamic to intimate, from everyday to ceremonial and ritual activities. Density creates a loss of (natural) qualities. Urban design and architecture can and must contribute to the neutralization of such losses by eliminating oppressive spatial effects and compensating them with allure. Putting together intelligent puzzles can produce high-quality interior and exterior domains. This study focuses primarily on this interaction between the public and private realms.

All sorts of cities are sources of inspiration for what I call the miracle of density. They contain exciting, bustling spaces full of variation and diversity. They have allure, but they also include unsuspected domains of intimacy. The significance of these spatial configurations usually lies in the motivations behind their creation, their history and their functions. A culture 'settles' in a network of proximities in order to enable all manner of lifestyles, with which we can (or cannot) identify, to relate to one another. This mutual proximity, with the market as its archetype, is the intrinsic quality and the appeal of cities. Accommodating it requires buildings. And building subsequently generates the ingenious system of public and multi-private spaces. Spaces whose conditions conform to the various activities to be expected and stimulated therein. It is precisely because this system is organized according to and expresses the values of a culture that a city is one of the most significant products of culture.

The city dweller is often part of multiple subcultural groups at the same time. The need for mutual proximity requires space for territories that overlap, places in the city (platforms) that different subcultures can use, simultaneously or at different times.

Urban diversity defines the quality and dynamism of a city. Firstly as a spatial system, of course. The mix of ingredients conditions the culture and the identity of a city. By accommodating different functions, the mix changes, and the specific character of the city emerges: a market town, royal city, garrison town, port city, university town, and all combinations thereof.

An analysis of the city should identify these different ingredients (port, park, buildings) of a city or urban tissue. Next, the quantity of the different ingredients should be examined in greater detail, especially in relation to one another. This mix is expressed in percentages. Then the distribution of these ingredients is looked at, for example in relation to the mesh of the urban tissue (the dimensions of city blocks, and therefore walking distances between different places). Finally, the superimposition, the concurrence of the various elements, is identified. Elements that are present simultaneously promote complexity and proximity, and therefore interaction between activities and events, and with it the degree of urbanity. Or at least its potential.

At the urban tissue level, we examine the composition and organization of public spaces. Streets determine the mesh of the urban network and with it the degree of penetration of the public domain into the private domain. Privatized space (from the palace and its grounds and the closed housing block to the free-standing building) is demarcated by streets, parks, water, squares, and so forth. In general, a few exceptions notwithstanding, space for access to the city coincides with the non-built space in the city.

Density in urban tissues is achieved, once an optimum balance between built and non-built space has been reached, by building deeper or stacking higher. Both operations result in a loss of certain qualities. However, a mutual proximity of urban activities, and therefore urban dynamism and efficient land use, are gained.

'The quality of density' is what matters to the city; in other words, are the physical possibilities of a location reduced or increased, made more diverse and more intensive, by the way in which buildings are arranged and compressed in relation to one another, and how does this relate to its use?

The study of density is not so much about maximizing density in terms of, say, floor space or people in general as it is about optimizing and guiding the mixture of the ingredients mentioned above. In our view, awareness of this data results in better, more ingenious urban tissues of built space interspersed with space left vacant. Instead of unconscious or experimentally discovered and copied solutions, this can lead to the development of an arsenal of 'genes and organs' for the urban body. The significance of this is political. It makes it possible to reasonably weigh interests against one another in order to serve diversity/heterogeneity and balance. This results in a more conscious programming of the issue of space allocation, using economic, cultural, architectural and urban-design instruments (including typologies). And this is sorely needed. For the use of space in the Netherlands is not growing gradually – it is accelerating at an exponential rate.

1
the website www.stedenvolruimte.nl has been set up to provide planners, urban designers, architects and students in various design disciplines with the results of the density research project of delft university of technology. the site offers spreadsheets into which any user may input his or her specific data. hypotheses can be tested and adjusted, and the inter-connected effects of decisions are made visible – an important tool at the scale of spatial planning and urban design, as well as that of architectural design.
the site also includes several interactive spreadsheets for density computations. there are animations in which various building patterns are displayed in 3-d. the blocklib (block library), as described on pp. 34-35, can be accessed from the site. the site also includes links to related websites, and it is open to a forum and commentary on the book. additions and new developments will also be listed on the site.

2
the density research project at delft university of technology, faculty of architecture, housing department, was conducted under the direction of professor in architecture related to practice rudy uytenhaak between 2003 and 2007. research assistance was provided by jeroen mensink, bart reuser, marijn schenk, saskia oranje, renske appel and simon de ruijter.

3
rudy uytenhaak obtained his degree from eindhoven university of technology, faculty of architecture in 1973, in architectonic urban design (under prof. d. apon and prof. w. quist)

If the country is to avoid silting up completely, more compact cities are imperative. This book aims to provide an impetus to a new way of thinking about urban densities. The first chapter, 'City Full of Spaces', describes, among other things, the research we have conducted at Delft University of Technology, which has resulted in a mathematical model and the Laws of Density derived from this. The mathematical model, incidentally, is available as a spreadsheet at the website www.stedenvolruimte.nl[1]

The work done at Delft University of Technology[2] can essentially be seen as making a science out of my design methods. Even as I was finishing up my studies I was looking for ways to increase the densities in particular planning areas.[3] In order to build more, but also better, housing than was actually required. Practically all my design sketches, in fact, include calculations that show how many dwellings a particular design variant produces. The chapter 'Drawing by Numbers' is about this practice-oriented research. The projects are listed in chronological order and were selected to illustrate particular problems that are inextricably connected to the creation of high densities. Designs that produce the largest quantities of housing units, after all, are not necessarily the best plans. The more dwellings, the greater the risk that this will come at the cost of, for instance, penetration of natural light into the dwelling or of the privacy of the occupants. The definitive designs must do more than eliminate all these risks. They must do more. They must compensate for the density created. This can only come in the form of more quality.

How this quality can be achieved is described in the third chapter, 'Spatial Quality, Compensation for Density'. The better we can describe this quality, the more quantitative analyses will be able to stimulate creativity and imagination.
The three chapters are all equally important. Without sufficient quality, density does not work – it is even dangerous. And quality can only be achieved by researching, by observing and most of all by playing with the puzzle pieces of floor plans and street maps and cross sections in order to achieve maximum syntheses.

urgency and instruments   **a city full of spaces**

**a city should bustle.
it should be full. full of people,
of functions, of movements.
in spite of its density and
fullness, it must not become
oppressive. in the dense
city, therefore, spaces are
imperative – spaces that
exude comfort, style and
perfection.**

As indispensable counterpoints to these grand spaces, the city also contains domains of intimacy. All of these spaces are significant and are laden with possibilities. They speak of life; they fill the city with stories.

How much space can be contained in relatively small pieces of urban tissue becomes clear during brief strolls around historic cities. They present a complete film

space in an urban tissue with a high density: oudegracht, utrecht

of impressions. Like Alice in Wonderland, one stumbles from one world into another. Take the city centre of Utrecht as an example: on a stroll down Oudegracht in the vicinity of the town hall, one walks along a meandering canal featuring different levels, with a combination of shops, offices, restaurants and cafés. Below, above, around the corner, behind a door, a window, on the roof, everywhere there is something to see. When a part of an urban tissue as condensed as this is torn down, it often turns out to have occupied a relatively modest area of land. The demolition of Les Halles in Paris, Kowloon City in Hong Kong and the Maupoleum in Amsterdam, for instance, revealed the gap between the perception of the 'world' of activities full of history and the spatial differentiation associated with it.

proximity
the paradox of 'space in density' is the secret of prosperous cities.

It serves as a neutralization and compensation for the inevitable loss of (natural) qualities engendered by density. This might identify the secret to a lively city, but it falls far short of explicating it. In order to design new cities with similar qualities, we have to conduct observations, typological explorations and fundamental research in historic cities. For much implicit know-how about how the miracle of density works is stored there, the product of centuries of intensive use of space. This does not mean we should succumb to the temptation of copying the objects of our study. Indeed, this is probably impossible. Our model cities, after all, were not designed to begin with. Their density, and with it their spatial layeredness, evolved in an almost organic way. They grew out of the human drive toward society, prosperity and diversion.

Because of this need for proximity, which can be called the essence of the city, both its population and the number of its functions increased. Growth in combination with a quest for safety and security automatically led to density, because growth had to occur within the city walls, which formed the unnatural and inflexible limits of the city. Building higher and deeper became necessary, and this made the urban tissue grow gradually denser. Both operations meant the automatic loss of certain qualities, but at the same time they produced a higher level of mutual proximity for urban activities, greater urban dynamism and more efficient use of land.

The open spaces in the cities came to be allocated according to the needs of their various subcultures. This resulted in ingenious spatial systems of public and collective spaces in which the encounter of the different subcultures led to synergy: the urban potential.

soho city, bejing

lucca

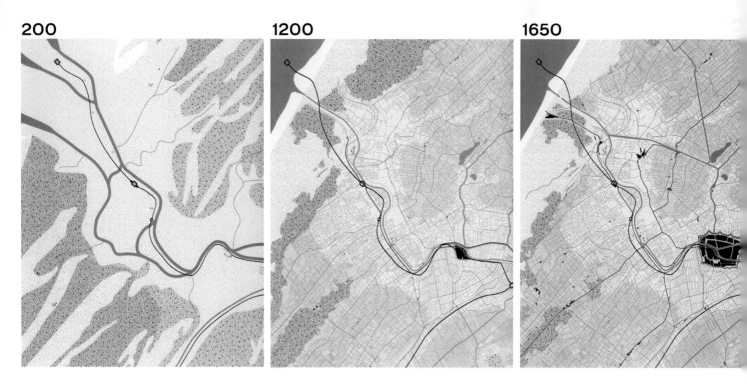

200 **1200** **1650**

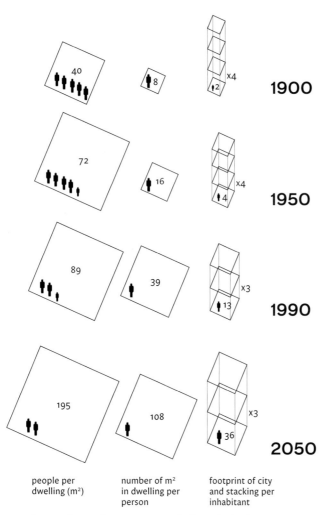

40	8	x4 / 2
		1900
72	16	x4 / 4
		1950
89	39	x3 / 13
		1990
195	108	x3 / 36
		2050

people per dwelling (m²) · number of m² in dwelling per person · footprint of city and stacking per inhabitant

increase in use of space per person in the netherlands

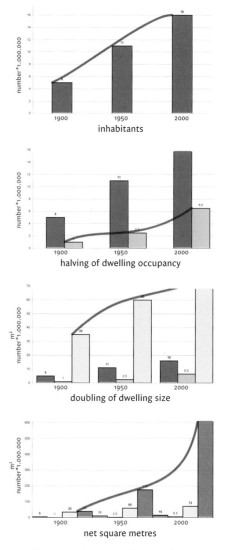

inhabitants

halving of dwelling occupancy

doubling of dwelling size

net square metres

total necessary housing surface area has increased by a factor of 16

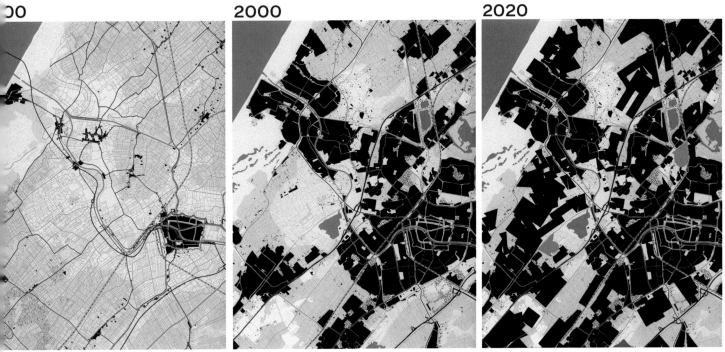

the leiden region underwent explosive growth during the twentieth century (source: limes atlas). right, the expected space requirements in 2020

explosion of the city: politics and urgency

Motivations for densification are no longer found in the city itself. Protective defence structures (fortified ramparts) have long since lost their function. Under the influence of more intensive mobility, technology and the declining economic importance of the surrounding agricultural lands, the boundary between city and landscape has become diffuse. New freedoms and possibilities have resulted in an erosion of the contemporary city and of the urban potential.

the cities of the netherlands have undergone explosive growth and have 'spilled over' an enormous amount of space.

Amsterdam, for instance, grew from 15 km² to 200 km² over the last 100 years, while its population grew by a mere 50 per cent (from 500,000 to 750,000 inhabitants). Had density remained constant, 22.5 km² would have sufficed.

The figures in the illustration below clearly show that per capita use of space, directly or indirectly, is responsible for an expansion of the urban area by a factor of 6.

simply put, half as many people live in homes three times as large as a century ago. when, on top of that, these homes are situated on twice as much land, this produces 2 × 3 × 2 = 12.

Finally, the population of the Netherlands has increased substantially. Whereas a little more than six million people lived in this country at the start of the twentieth century, the Dutch now number 16 million. All this means the use of space increased by a factor of 32 during the past century, explaining the evolution of cartographic data for the Netherlands over the last 100 years.

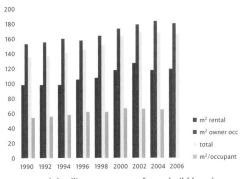

content and dwelling occupancy of new-build housing (source: cbs, leiden)

1900

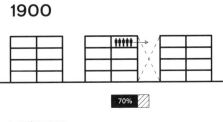

a century ago:
5 people per dwelling
short cross sections,
limited view (unilateral orientation),
shallow dwellings on narrow streets

2000

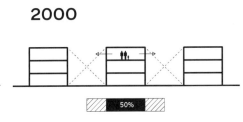

today:
2.3 people per dwelling
long cross sections,
open views (bilateral orientation),
deeper dwellings on broader streets

The political establishment continues to underestimate the effect of these factors. In general, it focuses on only one factor, forgetting that many, more or less independent factors affect growth cumulatively.

The consequence of this political inattention is that the use of space is not being consciously anticipated.

Say, for instance, that the population of the Netherlands does not grow, or grows only at a limited rate, and that the occupancy rate of homes decreases by another 20 per cent (from 2.2 to 1.8 residents per dwelling). In addition, dwellings will get larger.

1800

	1900	1950	2000	2050 suburb	2050 urban area
dwelling occupancy	5	4,5	2,3	1,8	1,8
net m²/dwelling	35	60	75	150	150
gross m²/dwelling	40	72	89	195	195
m²/person	8	16	38,7	108	108
open space in city	30%	35%	50%		
net built percentage	70%	65%	50%		
stacking factor	4	4	3		
FSi	1,9		0,75	0,5	1,2 (!)
net city/inhabitant	4,2 m²		51,6 m²	216 m²	90 m²
gross city surface area*	31 m²		275 m²		

indicative schedule of space needs development: around 2050, the surface area of an average suburban home will be 150 m²

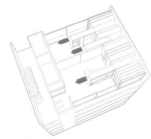

functionalist solution for m²
'wohnjockey', tobias huber, 2004

more probable reality in 2050:
spacious and loft-like

4
despite the large number of small dwellings in the cities, the lower limit for new construction now stands at around 90 m², and dwellings of 200 m² and larger have long ceased to be the exception. the dwelling size is contingent on such factors as economic development and the space needed for activities, such as working at home. what used to be perceived as luxury is increasingly identified as necessity. in the last 20 years, new-build dwellings have become 50 per cent larger (cbs-nvb). an average of 70 m² per person is no longer unusual. if in the next 50 years the demand for space is the product of 1.1 as many people (18.8 million), who want to live in homes twice as large, but will occupy their homes with 22 per cent fewer people (1.8 occupant per dwelling), the demand for space will increase by more than a factor of 3. (rudy uytenhaak in the book *grenzeloos wonen. europa verhuist*, 2008)

5
the research programme of delft university of technology, faculty of architecture – the research portfolio *context & modernity* – defines one of the six research questions as: how can we give the *physical space* of city and country those impulses that maintain or increase the attractiveness and quality of our cities? (urban dynamism implies a wealth of conditions of public\private, housing\ work, old\new). our answer: by offering models of different kinds of urban density that managed to combine proximity as well as privacy as a spatial quality with sustainable use of land.

no more existenzminimum
The efficient housing machines dreamt of by such architects as Le Corbusier, recently visualized in the ingenious wohnjockey pharmacy-cupboard dwelling by German architect Tobias Huber, in which all the separate functions (cooking, bathing, audio, television, fitness) are housed in pull-out cupboards set along the walls of an expansive room, is unlikely to catch on in a big way. This sort of efficiency is not appealing.

the expectation is that dwellings will actually double in size and reach 150 to 200 m². in our own homes we yearn not for a minimalist existence (existenzminimum), but for a diversity of atmospheres.
The space requirements of our homes will therefore increase by another factor of 2.5.[4]

making the best use of space

space occupied by shopping and housing is constantly increasing

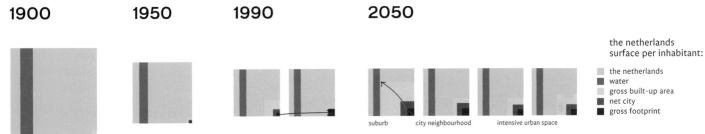

1900 **1950** **1990** **2050**

the netherlands
surface per inhabitant:

- the netherlands
- water
- gross built-up area
- net city
- gross footprint

suburb   city neighbourhood   intensive urban space

the personal space occupied per inhabitant of the netherlands:
in 1800, 2 million inhabitants had 17.000 m²/inh; in 1900, 5 million inhabitants had 7.500 m²/inh;
in 1990, 16 million inhabitants occupy 2.300 m² per inhabitant.
in red the expected development of the built footprint per inhabitant of the netherlands

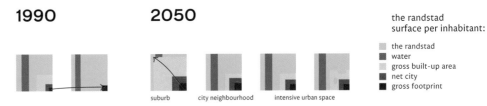

1990 **2050**

the randstad
surface per inhabitant:

- the randstad
- water
- gross built-up area
- net city
- gross footprint

suburb   city neighbourhood   intensive urban space

the personal space occupied per inhabitant of the randstad, the conurbation consisting of the
four largest dutch cities (amsterdam, rotterdam, the hague, utrecht) and surrounding areas.
in red the expected development of the built footprint per inhabitant of the randstad

we are also making more dynamic use of space outside the home.

A nineteenth-century mine worker spent 40 per cent of his time underground and 35 per cent at home, sleeping or eating. The remaining 25 per cent was for activities centred round the home. Today, workplaces are in use 25 per cent of the available time and, even then, it turns out, are only 50 per cent occupied; their occupancy rate is therefore 12.5 per cent. We spend another 35 per cent of our time sleeping. This therefore leaves more than 50 per cent, which we spend (individually or collectively, intensively or extensively) elsewhere. The trend towards more and more dynamic use of 'territory' seems irreversible.

science

All of this is shifting the balance between city and country. The landscape is fragmenting and the cities are wearing out. I have identified above the pressure to which this process is being subjected. We will have to develop strategies for containing the expanding private domain within the city, for how to accommodate it. Can architects and urban designers create cities full of space that turn this density not into confinement, but into freedom? To arrive at actual strategies, we need data. This need for data can lead to the emergence of an independent science.[5] We can draw a parallel to the medical science that grew out of human dissection.

This new science came about by accumulating more and more systematic knowledge about 'living tissues' and by linking consciousness, knowledge and precision. A comparison with mechanics is also illustrative. In this case, knowledge of forces resulted in exceptional achievements, with a more refined and more effective economy of materials.

Physical conditions are increasingly creating a need for similar achievements in the realm of the efficient management of space. This could lead to an economy of space. (What tension and compression are to mechanics, built and non-built space are to spatial density.)

This parallel goes further. Both sciences, mechanics and spatial economy, build on empirical know-how. For just as bridges made of lianas or the Roman aqueducts were early examples of the application of the knowledge of mechanics before a formal, theoretical science of mechanics even existed, our historic cities are rich sources of data about the density of spaces.

the economy of space should lead to an optimization of the use of space. not just as a sustainable principle in itself – exciting and exemplary – but also to vouchsafe the quality of an urban landscape of meaningful contrasts.

How do we carefully manage scarce space? How do we produce a vital dynamism for the city and landscape? How do we contribute to a continuity from old to new in terms of identity (intimacy, security, history) and dynamism (vitality)? What is the price of the suburban hybrid that emerges if everyone, with visions of luxury homes in Het Gooi or Wassenaar in mind, claims a pocket-size piece of the patchwork that is this country for him- or herself? And what are the alternatives? Is there such a thing as a public space that puts individual use of space into perspective, compensates for it and gives it meaning?

quantifying densities

Such questions can only be answered with good arguments if sufficient data are available. We have to know, for instance, how effective newly developed as well as historical urban tissues actually are. This can be done by quantifying density. The usual measure for density in (urban) residential areas is the number of dwellings per hectare (in Anglo-Saxon culture, the number of inhabitants per hectare).

although the concept of housing density – in its apparent link to a number of residents – appeals to the imagination, it is inadequate as a unit of measurement for a more scientific approach. several implicit variables cannot be distilled from this unit.

The housing density, for instance, only identifies the number of dwellings. The density of other functions, the size of the dwellings and the number of residents per dwelling is not made clear. And these factors are significant. It is far more verifiable, therefore, to express density in terms of the FSi, the Floor Space Index.

urban building types, increasingly dense

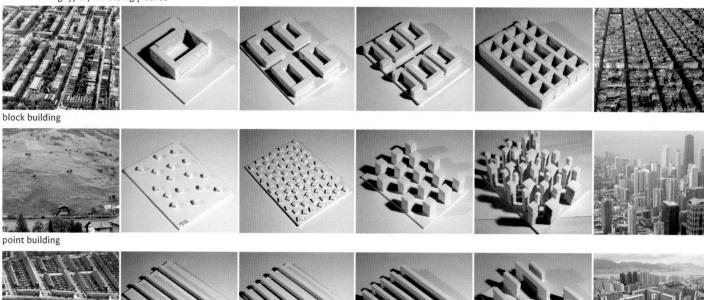

block building

point building

strip building

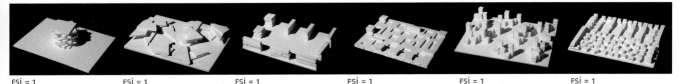

FSi = 1 FSi = 1 FSi = 1 FSi = 1 FSi = 1 FSi = 1

variations of stacking. four examples in which the FSi is 1 in different building patterns. exercises by students of delft university of technology

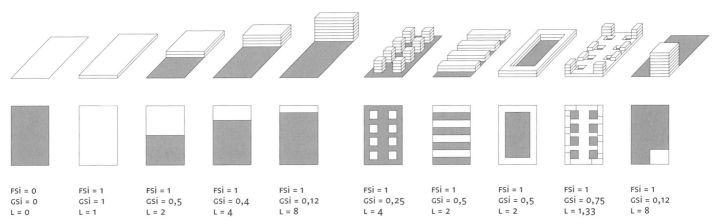

FSi = 0	FSi = 1	FSi = 1	FSi = 1	FSi = 1	FSi = 1	FSi = 1	FSi = 1	FSi = 1	FSi = 1
GSi = 0	GSi = 1	GSi = 0,5	GSi = 0,4	GSi = 0,12	GSi = 0,25	GSi = 0,5	GSi = 0,5	GSi = 0,75	GSi = 0,12
L = 0	L = 1	L = 2	L = 4	L = 8	L = 4	L = 2	L = 2	L = 1,33	L = 8

FSi = floor space index = total realized floor surface area in relation to ground surface area (in all these examples the FSi = 1)
GSi = ground space index = ratio between the footprint of the building and the available land
L = number of storeys

the floor space index (FSi) objectively represents how efficiently space is being managed. it is a ratio that indicates the total built floor space in proportion to the total area of the site. in numerical form it is equal to the built percentage times the stacking factor.

If we cover the entire available site with a single storey, the FSi is 1. If, for the sake of accessibility and natural light penetration for the spaces inside the buildings, we want to build on, say, one half of a site, we have to build two storeys in order to achieve the same index of 1.

In most measurements of actual situations, the FSi turns out to be less than 1. Values between 1 and 2 are already considerably urban. A 2, after all, means that the built surface covers 200 per cent of the whole site. Parts of Barcelona, with housing blocks of seven storeys set close together, approach an FSi of 4. Higher FSis are difficult to achieve. An exceptionally high value of 8, for instance, means that with a high percentage of built space of, say, 70 per cent (meaning only 30 per cent public space), an average of 16 storeys have to be built on 70 per cent of the footprint.

the fact that extremely high FSis are not feasible comes from the fact that buildings need 'air'.

If we consider a building mass as a volume of 'usable or functional' space – floor space with substance – every mass requires a sort of atmosphere to accommodate access, light and privacy. This space, along with the stackability of the units, determines the eventual packing.

soho city, bejing

net-gross series

Of course, the FSi is only a useful instrument if one site can be genuinely compared with another site on the same basis. This is possible when the sites for which the FSis are calculated are clearly demarcated.

for at every level of scale, the ratio of net to gross, that is to say the specific density of the building as well as that of the urban tissue, is different.

The lowest level of scale is that of the net house or residential building. The FSi value of the net house will usually be close to the stacking factor. Any voids, setbacks or cantilevered extensions lead to deviations from this. Zooming out one level, we reach the FSi of the net parcel. Here the required exterior space (the lot, more generally the allocated land) is factored in. Then comes the FSi of the gross parcel, with the necessary or presumed public area required for access and light penetration for the built volume.

The urban net fabric is one level higher in scale. This might be the housing block, the terrace of houses, the tower block or the individual dwelling, along with the immediate surrounding space. The length of a row of houses, for instance, affects the FSi because free space is provided at the end of the row that was not required for the other houses.

Next is the scale level of the neighbourhood, whereby a hierarchy of accesses, public greenery and facilities is factored in. After this comes the city borough and, if desired, the city, the region and, finally, the country. Each shift in scale means more ingredients – more 'orbits in the atmosphere around buildings' – are added, each of which takes up space of its own. The pure net yield, the density, decreases as parks, water, infrastructure, landscape, and so forth are factored in. Calculating back down to the level of the building, this means that every 100 m2 of Net Operational Floor Area (NOFA) requires an average 140 m² of Gross Floor Area (GFA). Depending on the stacking factor s, this produces a footprint of 140/s, so 70 m² for two storeys (s = 2). Stacking would therefore seem to have a linear impact on the size of the footprint.

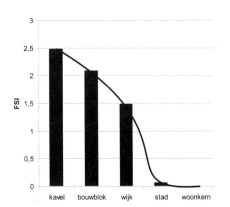

from parcel to region, each scale has its own FSi

parcel FSi = 2,5

building block FSi = 2,1

neighbourhood FSi (borneo island) = 1,5

borneo malaparte FSi sequence, zooming out from parcel to ever-larger urban area
control of space spillage: a contest between the architect and the urban planner in intensive use of space

This is too simple an approach, however. In general, it can be assumed that taller buildings require more tare space as a consequence of vertical transport: loads, pipes, access (lifts, corridors and stairs). Tare is the difference between net and gross space. To put it another way, the net floor area, because of tare structure, tare accesses, tare utilities, tare private exterior space (courtyards, yards, gardens), tare public exterior space (to accommodate the angle of obstruction and surface paving), tare neighbourhood facilities, greenery, etcetera – and so on at the city and regional levels – requires a series of allowances that yields the proportion of buildings to the gross quantity of space.

Let's say all the building stock in the Netherlands, at the urban tissue level, has an FSi of 1. The FSi of a residential district or city borough, because things like infrastructure, a park, a sports field and water are factored in, would be something like 0.5. For a big city, because of the presence of urban facilities, harbours, industry, and so forth, this produces an FSi of, say, 0.15.

the Netherlands	0.002
the Randstad conurbation	0.004
Amsterdam-Noord city borough	0.01
residential areas (CBS)	0.07
Amstelveen \ Almere suburban towns	0.08
Amsterdam Zeeburg including water	0.11
Amsterdam Zeeburg excluding water	0.3
residential areas Amsterdam	0.6
Amsterdam City Centre	0.8

Randstad = the conurbation consisting of Amsterdam, Rotterdam, The Hague and Utrecht and surroundings
CBS = Netherlands Bureau for Statistics

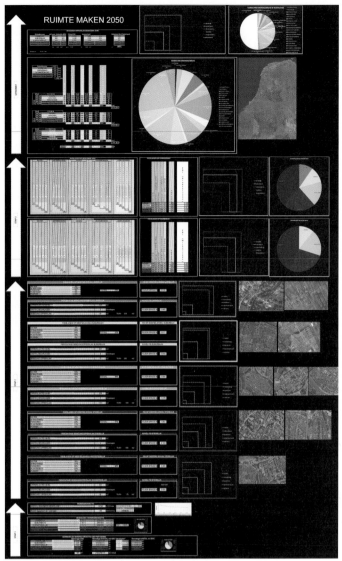

spreadsheet for calculating the density of the built-up area as a percentage of the netherlands with the parameters: inhabitants, dwelling occupancy and a telescope of FSi values. see also the website www.stedenvolruimte.nl

eastern harbour district FSi = ± 0,7

zeeburg FSi (excl. water) = 0,3

total amsterdam FSi = 0,2
(4,3/219 = gfa/area in km²)

tare telescope

The precise values of these different (per scale level) Floor Space Indices are of particular scientific importance in that they improve comparability among urban tissues. This makes more exact conclusions about capacity possible. The absolute values obtained are equally important in a social and political sense, however.

For they can be converted into an instrument for monitoring developments, clarifying selection scenarios and implementing these administratively in the wake of opinion forming and decision making. They provide insight into various programmatic distribution models and can thus clarify the sphere in which the space and the volume are organized. Are gardens and\or parks and\or landscape being created? What is that non-built space being reserved for? For whom and on what scale does this take place?

streets city   garden city   park city

tare telescope at the city level: in olive green, the gross urban space

tare telescope

■ footprint of net floor space
■ footprint of tare floor space > gross
■ parcel (assigned land including garden)
■ public highway
■ parking
■ public green space
■ water
■ city tare (infrastructure, work, amenties, etc.)

dunes
polder\agriculture
forest\nature reserves
river\lake
infrastructure
businesses
water
park
parking
streets
garden
footprint of tar floor space
footprint net floor space

differentiated tare telescope at the national level

land assets portfolio

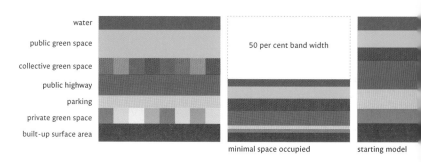

water
public green space
collective green space
public highway
parking
private green space
built-up surface area

50 per cent band width

minimal space occupied   starting model

tare telescope as planning instrument at the neighbourhood level

the 'tare telescope' can be used to map out and assess various urban design profiles. the tare telescope shows the ratio between net and gross floor space at the different levels of scale. when this tare telescope is expressed in segments in a bar chart for each level of scale, each area, a residential district for example, displays a different composition of segments of varying height. in analogy with topographic maps, there are red (built), green (non-built), blue (water) and white (infrastructure) segments.

If we look at the map dynamically, we can see that 'green is being displaced by red', 'green is being replaced by blue', and so on. When we expand the topographic map to the map of the city, it becomes evident that 'red' is made up of green, blue and white spaces, surrounded by red urban mass. Nolli's famous map of eighteenth-century Rome even turns the interior of public buildings, in terms of urban space, back to white.

The composite profile reveals much about the character of these areas. The proportion of private, public and landscape space will produce an entirely different profile for locations in the leafy, suburban and semi-rural area of Het Gooi than for a CIAM-inspired modernist urban development like Van Eesteren's Westelijke Tuinsteden (Western Garden City Districts) of Amsterdam.

We can compare city models with different space allocations across these levels of scale.

the distribution of profiles is of vital importance both from the standpoint of varied housing situations (options) and for the landscape diversity of the country.

The allocation of the available space budget, can be used to create different characteristics. In this the average value of that space budget will be important. Not as a solution, but as a norm or indicator of the parity of an area, or its deviation from it.

The tare telescope can also provide insight into the use of the land in another way. In this model, every inhabitant is assigned a personal territory. This is the number of square kilometres in a country divided by the number of its inhabitants, for example. If we assume 16.2 million Dutch people for an area of $34,600 \, \text{km}^2$, the average personal territory comes out to $2,136 \, \text{m}^2$ per capita. Imagine that the individual pieces of the country are then divided into various portions, for example landscape, water, infrastructure and city.

Of more particular interest is this can also be done at a lower level of scale. The residential district is then designed in collaboration with the parties concerned (city authorities, developers, users) with a focus on the question: 'What sort of image should the district have?'

the instruments can then be seen as a sort of mixing panel or slide-rule mechanism. If greater importance, and therefore a greater quantity of square metres, is ascribed to the private garden, less space is left over for water and green space.

This can define and programme the basic character of a residential district.

nolli's 'new map of rome' (1748) includes the interior of public buildings in the space of streets and squares.

minimum water

minimum public green space

minimum (automobile) access

minimum surface parking

maximum public green space

calculating and drawing graphics with rules

For planning and urban design projects, global computations using percentages and stacking factors are often sufficiently effective. They provide insight into the capacity and use intensity of the plan areas. For research into building types, a more in-depth examination of the profiles is crucial, because this allows not just square metres and the use of the land to be represented, but also cubic metres and the development of the volume. This is the more precise subject of this book.

our research is currently focused on the moment at which 'the red' of the flat, two-dimensional urban design of the planning map shifts into three-dimensional models.

The moment at which the blueprint traditionally turns into the Styrofoam model. The focus is on the interaction between this mass and the space it contains; the moment at which urban design and architecture become three-dimensional. This is the prelude to the art of transforming this material: 'filling gaps with space'.

we are examining here, for the benefit of functional density and diversity, the rules that are the foundation of the spatial density (of dwellings) in urban areas in relation to their spatial quality. we are primarily focused on insight into physical density.

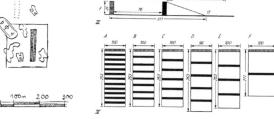

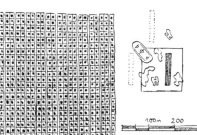

le corbusier, presentation of unité d'habitation. left, 500 house parcels 20×20 m, together 450×450 m, right, the high-rise with 500 dwellings on 160×160 m

walter gropius, strip construction (1929-30). comparison of building height variants: 2, 3, 4, 5, 6 and 10 storeys

modern architects absolutized stacking. 'light and air' were understood in too simple a parameter as the angle of obstruction to the penetration of light on the façade. this premise led to tall slabs and towers in empty fields

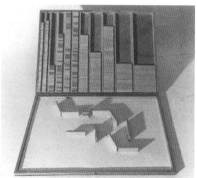

post-second world war model box, rotterdam urban planning department: standard reference housing construction in strips

amsterdam, chicago, osaka, lyon

density of significance and spatial quality are the ultimate objectives.

For most lay people, high density is synonymous with high-rise buildings. But just for them. Modernist architects like Walter Gropius and Le Corbusier based their argument for the park city on making the tower block an absolute. 'Light and air' were interpreted in too simple a parameter, namely the angle of obstruction to natural light penetration into the façade. This premise produced tall towers in empty fields. These areas were seldom interesting. They were too much of the same thing: monotonous in volume and space, with little differentiation. The physics of the space should instead be understood as the dynamic between density and emptiness.

The idea is to make dynamic use of the porosity of the built-up area, or formulated another way, the specific volume of the urban tissue.

for a city, a proper ratio between volume and space is crucial.

Not just as an absolute ('ideal') percentage, but particularly as an issue of distribution, whereby particles of mass and space are organized in optimum relation to one another. Distributions across various levels of scale overlap and in the process ultimately define the urban tissue.

with our research – all of the results of which can be consulted on the website as well as manipulated in a spreadsheet – we generated significant insights about densities. for instance, density turns out not to be a simple linear function of the stacking factor.
the computational model we developed shows what densities can be achieved with four building types (point, patio, strip and block buildings). this gives us a better grasp of the relationship between densities and natural light output, for example. the computational model features a number of important parameters.

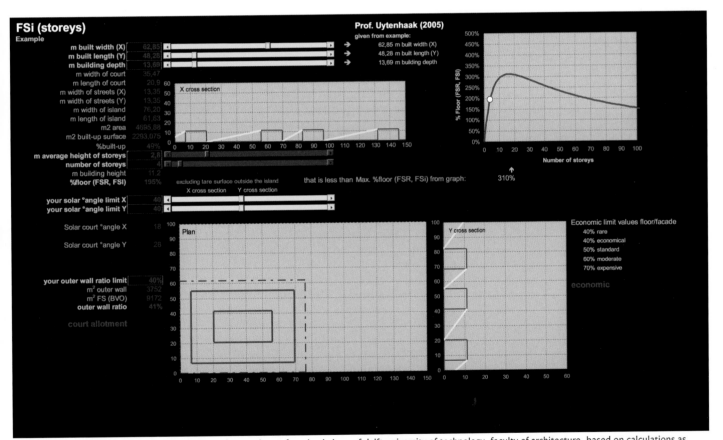

interactive spreadsheet on www.stedenvolruimte.nl set up by prof. taeke de jong of delft university of technology, faculty of architecture, based on calculations as explained in the chapters 'laws of density'. dimensions and storeys of a building block and angles of obstruction can be modified. the programme shows the attainable density and the façade index achieved

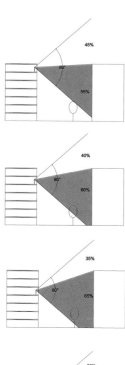

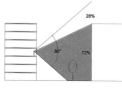

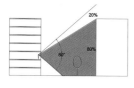

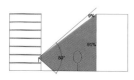

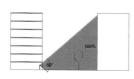

view and obstruction: the ratio of air\facing building on different storeys

6
the permeta *spacemate* develops a systematic approach to density at the urban design level.

the façade index is the ratio of the façade surface to the Gross Floor Area (GFA). the façade index is an important economic factor because the quantity of façade determines construction costs to a significant extent.

Optimizing the façade index, that is to say, keeping the quantity of façade per square metre of GFA as low as possible, makes economic sense. In this case, as in many others, such financial advantages run counter to the (spatial) qualities of buildings. The more façade a building has, the better the natural light penetration, the more spectacular the view and the more impressive the feeling of space. Spatial quality is determined to a certain extent by natural light output. Density can result in less natural light in the volumes, but it can also reduce the view of the sky. And this can create a sense of confinement. In the past, rules of thumb were set up to determine how densely the city can be built up and still allow adequate natural light to come into buildings. Systematically collected data, however, is lacking.

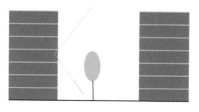

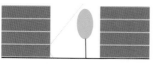

with equal angles of obstruction, very different view and field of vision

At Delft University of Technology (TU Delft) we have conducted research in collaboration with the departments of Building Physics and Urban Design (Permeta)[6] in order to arrive at more sensible considerations in the production of new urban volumes on the basis of their light output.

this answered such questions as: 'how does increasing density affect light in the exterior and interior?', 'is it more effective to stack than to deepen?', 'what improvements are possible?' and 'what effects do ceiling heights and reflections have?'.

To limit the definition of the problem and to make in-depth research possible, we initially focused on the 'urban design shell'. This is the total of floors and dwelling-separating walls. The façade is imagined as entirely open. We were primarily interested in the penetration depth of natural light in terms of light levels in lux. Qualities such as uniformity or instead contrast in luminance variations require supplementary research.

When storeys are stacked, the street wall gets taller, or, from the standpoint of light, the 'canyon' gets deeper, and it gets darker at street level. More or less reflection along the façade may affect the ultimate value of the light down below, but less contact with the sky primarily restricts the starting point for the interior, in other words the starting value of natural light immediately behind a completely open façade is decreased.
In addition to this external obstruction of the façade, the internal angle of obstruction is also significant for the interior:

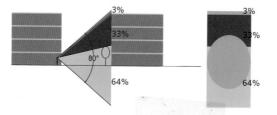

compilation of view on different **storeys with an 80°** vertical field of vision

spaces with higher ceilings bring light deeper into the building and increase contact with the sky. Here too, reflections from the walls are important for the output of this light. Room proportions and the reflective values (light/gloss) of the walls can optimize light quality.

The angle of natural light is the product of the internal and external angles of obstruction, that is to say the angle between the lower and upper shadow (see illustration) and determines how deep the light can penetrate into the room. This makes it indicative of the quality of the ratio between space and mass.

The data collected makes it possible to better study such existing and somewhat simplistic rules of thumb as 'make the angle of obstruction no greater than 45 degrees' and 'a room can be twice as deep as it is high'. The balance between the internal and external angle of obstruction is different in low-rises than in high-rises, for instance. This undercuts all the simplistic linear outputs and applications of the rules of thumb.

light, lower shadow and upper shadow

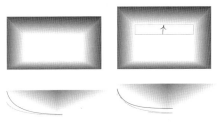

light\view
decrease in light in the cross section and the impact on this by the improvement of external (left) or internal (right) angle of obstruction: more light at the façade or at the rear of the room

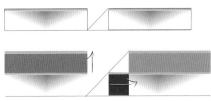

building depth d = 4 × ceiling height v

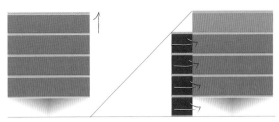

the effect of an angle of obstruction of 45° on stacking: in order to achieve 1 extra storey the site has to be expanded in equal measure to the ceiling height. in the step to 5 storeys (where v/d = ¼) making 4 floors deeper would have produced the same increase in surface area

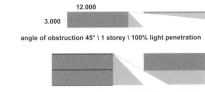

angle of obstruction 45° \ 1 storey \ 100% light penetration

angle of obstruction 45° \ 2 storeys \ 41% light penetration

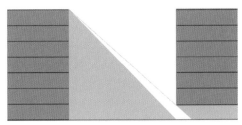

angle of obstruction 45° \ 7 storeys \ 26% light penetration

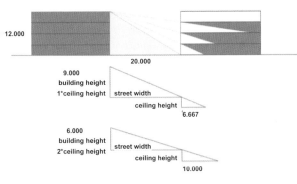

lower shadow and upper shadow;
see also the 'laws of density' chapter

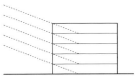

light penetration from the open field: equal ceiling height produces a constant distance of natural light penetration

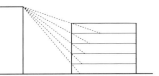

light penetration with an angle of obstruction: equal ceiling height produces a variable distance of natural light penetration

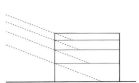

light penetration from the open field: variable ceiling height increases the distance of natural light penetration

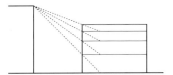

light penetration with an angle of obstruction: variable ceiling height produces a constant distance of natural light penetration

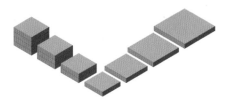

densification by stacking   densification by expanding

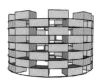

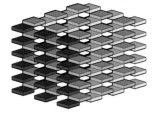

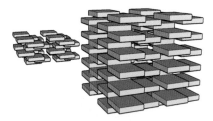

density studies by students of delft university
of technology, faculty of architecture

laws of density

density, a high FSi value, is achieved by stacking storeys on a base with a high built percentage, such as full-surface or fringe buildings.
The building depth and the pattern of built/non-built space determine the built percentage. The pattern of built/non-built space, the stacking factor and the ceiling height determine the angle of obstruction.

the built percentage, stacking factor and angle of obstruction are the primary determinants of density.
When the angle of obstruction and the building depth are equal, the increase in the FSi levels off as storeys are stacked. The pattern of built and non-built space, along with the ceiling height, determine the façade index.

the façade index defines the potential relationships between inside and outside, such as light and views. the angle of obstruction externally determines (outside) the upper limit of this potential. the angle of natural light determines the depth of light penetration into the interior.

the following rules are an attempt to identify these factors in order to develop intelligent urban tissues in which density and primary spatial quality can be optimized.

1
Density (FSi) is increased by stacking as well as by making buildings deeper. Combining higher and deeper buildings produces higher returns than either one alone

2
If buildings are stacked higher or made deeper, with the angle of obstruction remaining constant, the increase in the FSi levels off rather than progresses linearly: returns diminish. The formula for profile density is as follows: $FSi/m^1 = N*d/(d+s)$. In the case of an angle of obstruction of 45°, a tangent of 1 means that $s = N*v$ (street width = number of storeys * ceiling height), making the formula: $FSi/m^1 = N*d/d+N*v$ (N = number of storeys, d = building depth, s = street width, v = ceiling height).

3
If building depths, angles of obstruction and stacking are equal, patio patterns, based on their built percentage, have the highest FSi, tower blocks the lowest. If the depth is corrected to produce an equal façade index, the FSis of strips, housing blocks and patios are equal. Point buildings score somewhat lower.

4
Point building arrangements, optimized in 'checkerboard' form, produce the highest FSi.

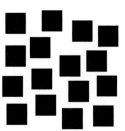

optimized point building in a 'checkerbord' of five overlaid patterns. the spacious intersection between the four big blue towers now contains four extra smaller towers

5

The FSI is independent of scale: the FSi and façade index remain equal in the case of proportional increases in ceiling heights and building depths (with a constant angle of obstruction). In the case of a limited building height and an equal Gross Floor Area, shallow buildings with lower ceilings produce a slightly higher FSi.

6

A greater external angle of obstruction increases the FSi and lowers the potential output of natural light inside. Making a building deeper while the angle of obstruction remains constant also results in an increase in the FSi and a decrease in the actual natural light output per Gross Floor Area. The FSi increases slowly in the case of a deep building combined with a large angle of obstruction. Building deep buildings with a high angle of obstruction (over 30 degrees) decreases the necessity of positioning buildings close to one another, since the FSi increase is not linear in such cases. With smaller angles of obstruction and fewer layers, the increase remains constant

7

If the angle of obstruction is equal, the penetration depth of natural light is greater when the street width is smaller. The theoretical penetration depth of natural light = street width * ceiling height / (adjacent building height – height of individual ceiling with respect to ground level) (the angle of natural light is equal to the angle of obstruction of the storey above).

The **actual** penetration depth and light output diminish as a result of possible obstructions in the façade and because of the boundary walls and the reflection value of all obstructions (absorption percentage). To achieve a constant penetration depth for storeys stacked on top of one another, the ceiling height must be differentiated (see illustration).

8

The lit surface area of a building is in linear proportion to the Façade Index.

9

In the case of limited obstruction, a lower ceiling is more effective for the ratio of floor area exposed to natural light and the associated façade index. In the case of an angle of obstruction greater than 30 per cent or 45 per cent, there is little to no significant difference in the percentage of floor area exposed to natural light in spaces with a high but narrow façade or a low but wide façade.

For an elaboration of these laws, see the theoretical section at the end of this book.

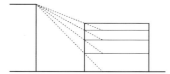

light penetration with an angle of obstruction: variable ceiling height produces a constant distance of natural light penetration

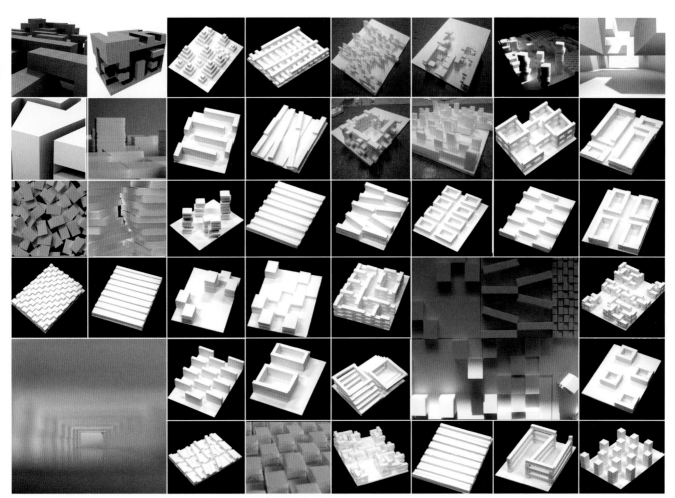

density studies by students of delft university of technology, faculty of architecture

coral: optimum
light efficiency

sketch models by students of delft university of
technology, faculty of architecture

toposphere

These rules of density are based on theoretical models. These models lead to recommendations and design projects. In addition, the comparison with actual urban tissues will result in more verifiable data. More field work would have to be conducted in order to test the effectiveness of given design decisions. We should find out what the ultimate ratio between 'red', 'green' and 'blue' is, how the quality of the public space is perceived and what the ratios of NOFA to GFA are in residential districts. What is the actual use of space and what is the physical space shortage?

this research is clearly not intended to reproduce successful residential districts.

This is too often the case currently, with detailed zoning plans supplemented with visual quality plans in order to define the desired character. The use of visual quality plans in these instances is far too limited. It is too oriented towards reproducing the familiar, with excessive emphasis on existing forms, instead of striving to be generatively conditioning by aiming for quality.

this research should instead result in a catalogue in which typologies and quantifications of various building forms in urban tissues are identified: types, programmes and defined spatial quality.

By qualifying spatial qualities for (concentrated) housing construction with numbers where possible and with indicators (from **++** to **– –**, as in consumer studies) otherwise, it becomes possible to make the density of different plans comparable, both quantitatively and qualitatively. They contribute to the planning and the regulation of urbanization processes. For new plans, this produces an indication of building proportions per number of square metres to be realized (in other words, FSi). In this way, the domain of urban housing density can be made more open to intuition. Better insight in the specific volume of the urban tissue can produce new elements for the toposphere.

The toposphere is essentially the last of the shells around the earth as described in geology. The outermost shell, out to the edge of space, is called the atmosphere. The lowest layer of the atmosphere, closest to the earth's surface, is called the troposphere. This is the shell in which man breathes and in which weather unfolds. The top layer of the earth's crust is called the lithosphere. In the zone in which the troposphere and the lithosphere intertwine, man builds and lives. We call this space or living sphere the toposphere. It consists of a collection of spaces at human scale. These are the places in which man spends his time, from the underground mine and the cellar up to the penthouse and the office tower.

Differentiating and intensifying the toposphere creates a division of spaces, and therefore of spatial density. Just as the ploughed soil of the field or the wall of the intestine expands the space of the border zone and creates more surface area, so we plough, as it were, the toposphere – to make it porous. The folds and hollows in the toposphere maximize the contact surface for interaction. This porous layer reaches its maximum thickness in the layeredness of the most urban areas. Often with underground layers of cellars, tunnels, cables and mines.

We also encounter the spatial qualities of the surface on a smaller scale, that of buildings. When a surface – more or less porous or layered – is given depth, this produces characteristics such as the absorption of sound and heat. The porous surface of the building can also resist wind, light and moisture. Urban design and architecture are both exercises in opening and filling mass, space and material. In the process they create space, each at its own level of scale.

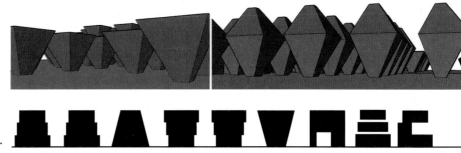

set back   small footprint   voids\hollows

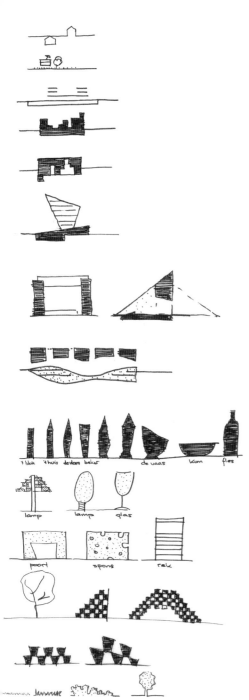

manipulating volumes: porosity and profiles

space is thus created by hollowing out, expanding, deepening, connecting and stacking volume.

Spatial differentiation is created by divisions in space, for example with walls and floors. We easily associate both with the concept of density. You can stack floors, literally creating more usable surface area; walls close up space and allow different functions and activities to occur independently and yet in proximity to one another.

the volumes studied in the computational model – point, patio, block and strip construction – are essentially simple extrusions of floor plans or cross-sections, of stacking mass upright or squeezing out cross sections. these volumes can be moulded, tapering upward for instance. they can be perforated with air, pierced by other volumes, or transformed.

You can curve towers or strips. Rotate them along the longitudinal axis, expand them or instead carve them up.

If we take it a step further, the high-rise can be tipped over and laid out like a letterbox on the ground, as a slab structure, or other 2-D linkages. That plane can be curved in turn. Or you can stagger volumes on top of one another instead of straight up, in two but also in three dimensions. Like a three-dimensional checkerboard, for instance. Or even more dynamically, by simultaneously rotating them. This creates more empty space under the mass, in the form of portals or extra-high spaces. In a more or less inverse process, we can start with the mass instead of the space. Adaptation then consists, as it were, of working in the opposite direction and piercing the urban mass with holes. By positioning these holes strategically, like the shafts in a pyramid, a porous urban tissue like a sort of sponge, coral or Swiss cheese can be created, built by perforation. Finally, if we zoom in down to the scale of the building, an entirely new layer of density emerges in this hollowing-out method when we realize that urban mass is not made of Styrofoam, but of floors with specific heights. Our study into the relationship with natural light penetration demonstrates that ceiling height is connected to building depth. When this is applied, a differentiation of floors with denser or more open packing emerges. This also varies according to function. As a result of this differentiation, the heterogeneity and dynamism of the urban tissue increase even further. This differentiation is usually inspired by functionality and spatial perception.

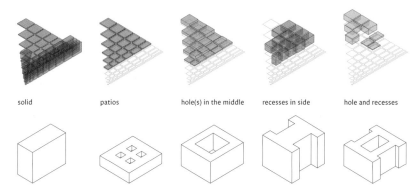

solid patios hole(s) in the middle recesses in side hole and recesses

block library: in the progressive sequence of possible building volumes from 5 × 5 × 3 m to 50 × 50 × 50 m,
880 positions are conceivable and have been filled in by students with possible housing linkages:
at every stage of block growth, different strategies of saving are effective within the matrix (see colours)

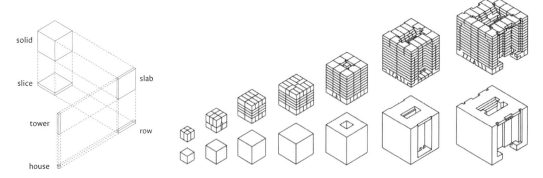

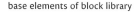

solid

slice slab

tower row

house

base elements of block library

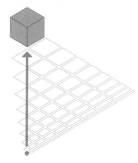

the extremes of the block library:
5 × 5 × 3 m tot 50 × 50 × 50 m

7
see the article by bart reuser and rudy uytenhaak,
'prototypes or series', in *de architect* november 2006,
pp. 20-23.

8
see also the dwelling typology on the inside front
cover of this book.

blocks library: typology
a matrix for housing typologies

We initiated this study because we are
convinced that new answers are needed.
We can no longer build the way we have
over the past several decades.

**we have to make it attractive
not to cover the whole country
with building developments.
cities will therefore have to
become denser within their
own limits once again, but in
such a way that their quality
and therefore attractiveness
are increased.**

This requires additional effort by all parties.
After all, it is economically simpler to turn
a pasture into a residential development
than to build inside an existing urban tissue.
Returning to building inside the city means
adding new elements that might provide
renewed impetus to the hollowed-out
city, that might enrich its dissipated urban
building vocabulary.

**for this we need a range of
new 'genes' and 'organs'
for new urban tissues.**

Not only because the location demands it,
but certainly because its changing use is
crying out for it.

**the standard house
and the standard high-rise
are undergoing significant
changes. architects can
contribute to the development
of a new palette.**

By taking existing settings and buildings
apart again and again, and reconstructing
them in new projects, the architect trains his
powers of imagination. This is done not only
by developing examples, but particularly
by drawing abstractions from them. In the
process, knowledge can be garnered on a
conceptual level and analysed in order to
arrive at essential alternatives.

**research has been conducted
at tu delft in order to increase
systematic knowledge of the
capacity of (housing) volumes
and new building typologies.
these are typologies that have
to be located in between the
standard types, as it were.**

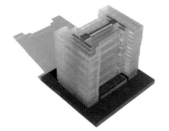
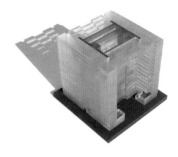

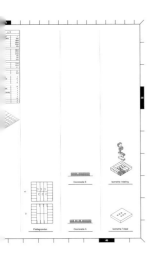
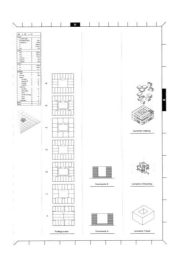
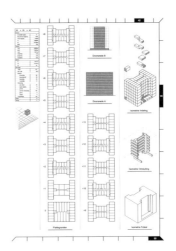
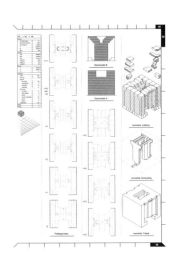

to this end a three-dimensional matrix was developed, in which 880 volumes were analysed systematically.

The smallest is 5 × 5 × 3 m and this volume is increased in increments of 5 × 5 × 3 up to the maximum volume of 50 × 50 × 50 m, comparable to the increments in the computational model described above, but at the building level. Subsequently, the volumes produced were subjected to requirements involving natural light penetration and the most efficient way of providing access.[7] These two requirements were self-evident. As far back as 1978, in the book *Modern Housing Prototypes*, Roger Sherwood described buildings using these two criteria. He argued that the dwelling is organized in terms of orientation and the residential building in terms of access.

To provide timely use of the matrix, a three-dimensional navigation system has been developed and is available on the website, through which volumes – building types – can be easily selected. Individual efficiency is clearly displayed by the data sheets and graphics, making it easy to quickly compare different types.

the programme produces a new palette of sensible hybrid residential buildings. hybrid in the sense that they cannot be assigned either to one standard type or the other. they are somewhere in the twilight zone between standard types. to meet the new demands of users and at the same time make the city liveable again and as richly varied as before, we will have to venture into this domain of the hybrid types.

And actually this has been happening for some time.

If we put a few of the plans of the last decade alongside one another, we notice that they include all sorts of buildings that no longer fit in the box of standard solutions of urban designers. Back-to-back patio types on Borneo Island and super-blocks on Java Island (both redeveloped artificial islands in Amsterdam's Eastern Harbour District), tall patio blocks on the Funen site in Amsterdam, massive towers on the Müllerpier in Rotterdam.

All are hybrid types that cannot be easily categorized as one typology or the other. It's not a tower, but it's not a block either; it's a block, but there are patios in it. We developed these building types based on insight, experience and intuition. The process involved painstakingly figuring out a puzzle of floor and ground plans to achieve the optimum density on the one hand and of course to give the dwellings adequate qualities on the other.

in principle, density must not come at the expense of the enjoyment of the home. in fact the quality of the dwelling, the residential building and the surrounding public space should provide compensation for the density that has been reached.

Natural light penetration, access, views, privacy and the quality of the (semi-) public space are therefore always important pieces of our puzzles. Using a number of examples, we now want to show how we construct these puzzles and how we try to create cities with high densities yet full of spaces.[8]

practice

drawing by numbers

low-rise, high-density linked dwellings;
block of flats with communal entrance

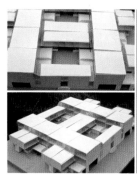
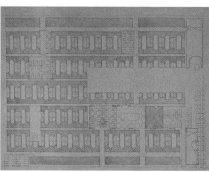
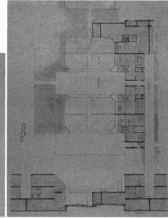

typology study of low-rise, high density dwelling for a fictitious site:
studies and model as part of graduation project from the eindhoven university of technology architecture faculty

typology study **low-rise in high density,** 1972
plan for the **kinkerbuurt,** amsterdam 1972-1973
dwellings per lateral metre of street
**80 to 140 dwellings\hectare
extrusion model from the cross section;
density used to counter overflow out of
amsterdam to growth cores elsewhere**

This plan is part of a series of housing studies
into intensive low-rise buildings: the top design
was for a graduation project at Eindhoven
University of Technology, the other three are
redevelopment studies for the Kinkerbuurt
area in Amsterdam Oud-West. The plan for the
Kinkerbuurt offers an alternative to the overflow
sites (Purmerend and Almere). The objective is
to build good dwellings in a density not much
lower than that of the Kinkerbuurt at the time.
The city, however, had proposed a 40 per cent
reduction in the number of dwellings. In order
to achieve a high density, the cross section
has been intensified, as it were, and includes
forms of habitation for different target groups.
The linear building arrangement can gradually
regenerate the old blocks. An alternative plan
is based on a non-linear building arrangement,
but this represents a major departure from the
urban-design concept. Both the Kinkerstraat
and the Jacob van Lennepkade, after all, require
strong street façades. In the final plan, the
linear and non-linear building arrangements
have been combined, creating a more introvert
yet spacious living environment between two
strong façades. Research into urban density has
become increasingly urgent over the last 30 years,
as well as a recurring theme in all the work of
Rudy Uytenhaak's firm.

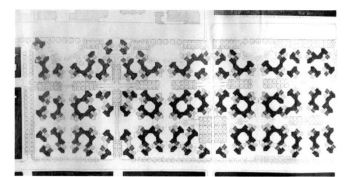

kinkerbuurt plan 1: 276 dwellings + 57 professional spaces or shops,
density 100-121 dwellings\hectare

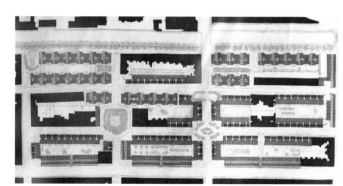

kinkerbuurt plan 2: 378 dwellings + approx. 6 shops,
density 135 dwellings\hectare

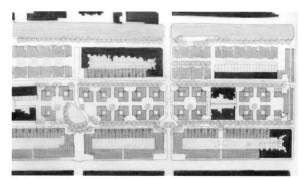

kinkerbuurt plan 3: 450 dwellings + 6 (or more) shops,
density 140-160 dwellings\hectare

typology study of low-rise, high density dwelling: the dwelling forms the link to a narrow accessway. the gardens are perpendicular to this, with the garden path and the special routes for children as the connection to the green zones in the plan (perspectives 2008)

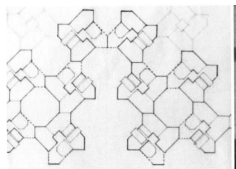

kinkerbuurt plan 1: detail of floor plan, model

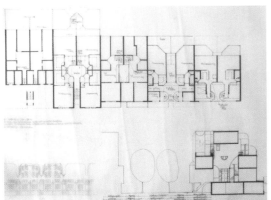

kinkerbuurt plan 2: detail of floor plan and cross section

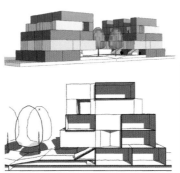

cross section and perspectives (2008)

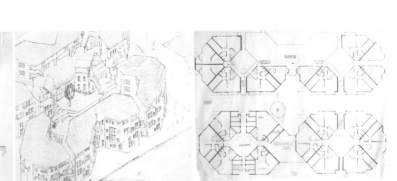

kinkerbuurt plan 3: combination of strips and residential blocks   sketch of residential blocks with first-storey courtyard, map of residential block

canal house	gallery flat	tower flat
9 dwellings (template)	20 dwellings (template)	46 dwellings (template)
946 m² GFA	1,870 m² GFA	4,512 m² GFA
4.5 FSi net parcel	3.9 FSi net parcel	8.0 FSi net parcel
3.3 FSi gross parcel	3.0 FSi gross parcel	4.4 FSi gross parcel
0.8 GSi net parcel	0.4 GSi net parcel	0.7 GSi net parcel
0.6 GSi gross parcel	0.3 GSi gross parcel	0.4 GSi gross parcel
stacking factor 5.6	stacking factor 10	stacking factor 12

weesperstraat building complex
amsterdam city centre, 1980-1992
repairing an urban intervention
205 dwellings and 15 office spaces
historical context
connection to canals
noise reduction
creating a plaza and many dwellings

The construction of the metro and the construction of the Weesperstraat punched a sizable hole in the canal structure of Amsterdam's city centre on the east side of the Amstel.
The 12-storey diamond-shaped tower block and the rectangular 10-storey building on the other side of the Nieuwe Kerkstraat fit in, in terms of scale, with the metropolitan character of this urban intervention. They had to be connected, however, to the smaller-scale structure of the existing, individual canal houses. For this reason, the canal façade, at the corner, has been given architectonic priority in both size and expression. The tower block is therefore set back from the corner and features four dwellings per storey.
In the more rectangular building, the lower-level dwellings are accessed by stairwells and the top six storeys by two galleries.
The position of the apartment buildings along the Weesperstraat is dictated to a significant extent by the noise stress on the façade. The buildings, which contain both flats and offices, are therefore set back from the street, forming a plaza. Two underground parking levels extend from one canal to the other.

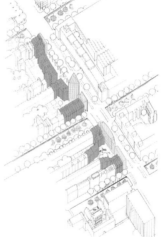

canal side　　　　　　　　　　　　　　　　garden side

sketches for the dwellings on the canals: deep blocks (as before), with living quarters on the canal side and sleeping quarters on the garden side. light yards allow light to penetrate deep into the building. staggered balconies look out over the communal garden

scale of individual houses and large scale of weesperstraat turned into a 'metropolitan' thoroughfare

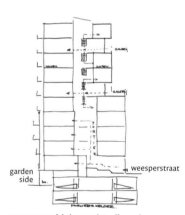

garden side　　　　　weesperstraat

access combining stairwells and galleries, in order to limit the number of flats per lift and to increase social control

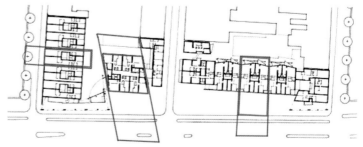

after the radical urban intervention for the construction of the metro and the major traffic artery into the city centre, the connection of the new buildings with the existing canal houses had to be subtly tuned. In the middle, the passage to the nieuwe kerkstraat, towards the amstel

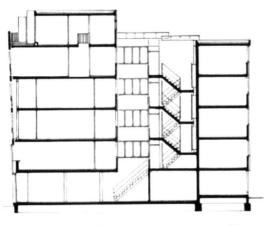

cross section of dwellings on the nieuwe prinsengracht

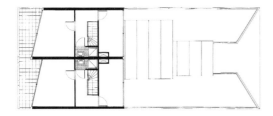

floor plans of 25-m-deep dwellings on the nieuwe prinsengracht

the large buildings on the busy weesperstraat. the residential buildings that connect to the canal houses have been adapted, in terms of scale and detailing, to the historical construction. office blocks form the sound-absorbing 'ends' directly on the weesperstraat and 'repair' as much façade length as possible along the canal

N40
94 dwellings (template)
(incl. commercial space)
10,076 m² GFA
3.6 FSi net parcel
1.8 FSi tissue
0.7 GSi net parcel
0.3 GSi tissue
stacking factor 5.3

N41
9 dwellings (template)
(incl. commercial space)
1,125 m² GFA
5.0 FSi net parcel
3.1 FSi gross parcel
1.0 GSi net parcel
0.6 GSi gross parcel
stacking factor 5

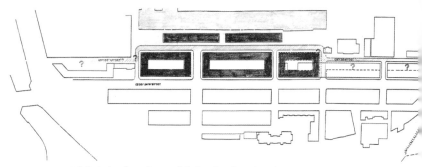

original plan from the spatial planning department:
elimination of the existing street pattern

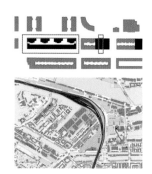

residential blocks czaar peter \ conradstraat
amsterdam, 1980-2005
natural light in shallow \ deep linear dwelling types
N40: shallow strip and 4 residential blocks
N41: two blocks, each 24 m deep

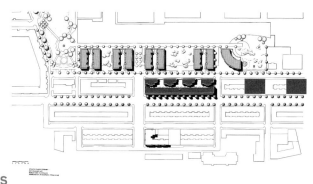

definitive proposal by Uytenhaak and the czaar peterbuurt conservation and restoration committee: strip N40 on the czaar peterstraat and 4 lower blocks on the conradstraat. the street pattern is retained. right, the 24-m-deep blocks at N41, with façades on both streets

The old speculation-built structures dating from around 1900 had to make way for new buildings in the 1980s. The city initially wanted to alter the depth of the blocks in the Czaar Peterbuurt. Residential blocks 10 to 12 m deep would be situated on either side of the 18-m-deep gardens – in order to get as much natural light into the dwellings as possible. This would, however, change the existing network of streets into a structure of streets blocked at the ends by new blocks. 'Counterproposals' were submitted in collaboration with the Czaar Peterbuurt Conservation and Restoration Committee to show that the existing pattern could be retained: instead of using off-the-shelf standard urban design, the spatial issues were resolved through the architecture and the dwelling design. The alternative plan retains the existing street pattern. It is based on blocks only 24 m deep. At N40 the desired density and urban aspect with continuous street façades is achieved by placing separate blocks behind a strip; at N41 this is done by building up the entire depth.

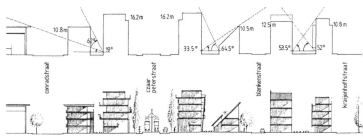

studies into differentiated streets and the resulting angles of obstruction

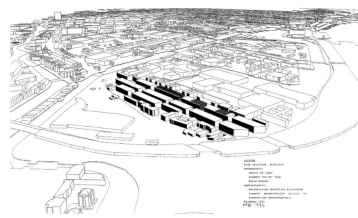

the marked blocks N40 and the two residential blocks N41 in their context

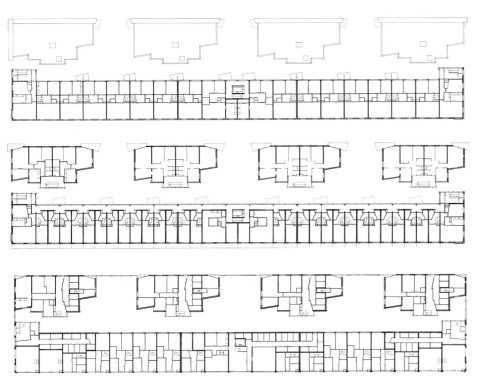

study into types and numbers of dwellings

N40 floor plans: ground floor, 3rd and 4th floors

as in the historic city, high-ceiling lower storeys with a lot of glass allow natural light deep into the block: office and commercial spaces

N40 model

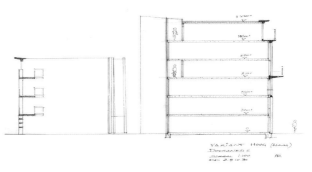

sketch of N40 cross section

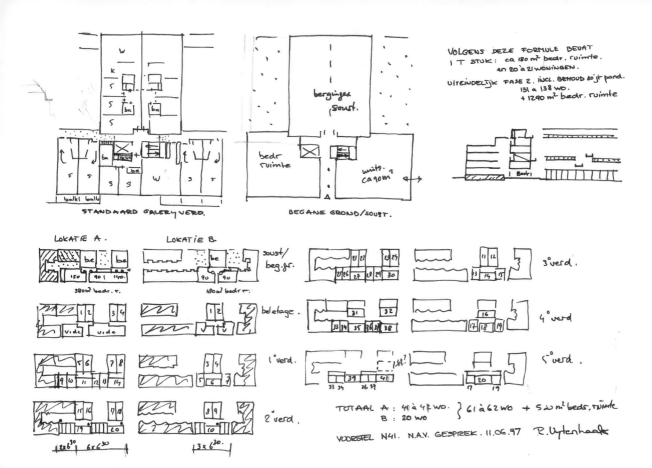

earlier studies for the infill of the two N41 locations, with T-sections

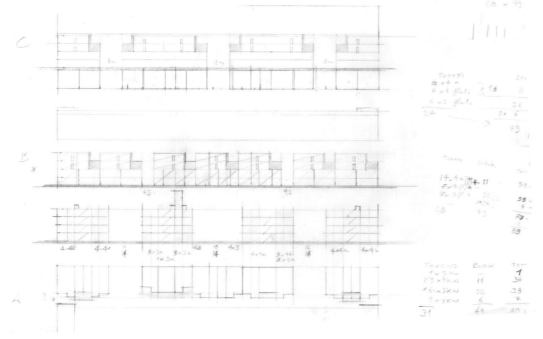

study into the distribution of N41, with capacity calculations in the margin

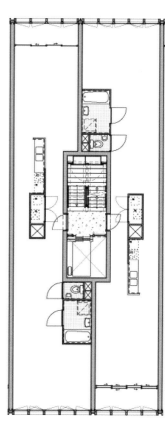

dwelling floor plans

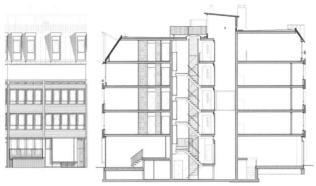

conradstraat, façade · cross section with light yard and stairwell

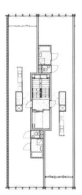

top floor with roof terrace

floor plan of upper-storey dwellings

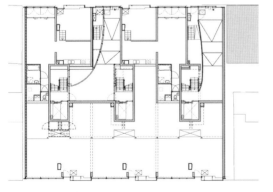

floor plans of ground floor

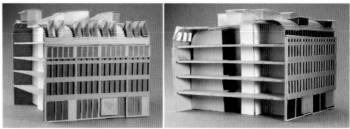

cross section of model with centrally situated stairwell and light yard, and therefore no access to the façade

the striking dormers on the conradstraat are made of glass on one side; they are spacious and open and yet provide privacy

czaar peterstraat

streetscape of N41 on the czaar peterstraat with a lot of glass on the ground floor. above this, a solid, classic brick façade because of the deep niche, yet as much light and view as possible by positioning the brickwork in front of the window frame

walk-up flats & gallery flats
10 dwellings (template)
738 m² GFA
2.0 FSi net parcel
1.6 FSi gross parcel
0.4 GSi net parcel
0.3 GSi gross parcel
stacking factor 5.3

early sketch of the building

droogbak residential building
amsterdam city centre, 1986-1989
privacy in urban context
noise prevention
using balconies to prevent others looking in
providing light

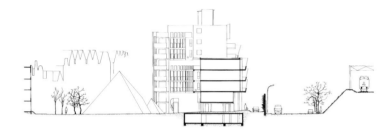

the cross section shows the complexity of the site: the building is located alongside a busy road and there is a public plaza behind the building

The Droogbak residential building is situated alongside a busy road and right next to the railroad tracks. It is located on the edge of the historic city centre and right before the old harbour front. By acting as a noise barrier, the building creates a small quiet plaza on the city side, with a sports court and playgrounds for children. This created new space in the city. Access is located on the busy traffic side. The building consists of walk-up flats as high as regulations allowed, in order to make the relationship between the dwellings and the street as direct as possible. Above this, several galleries for elderly residents in communal arrangements were built.

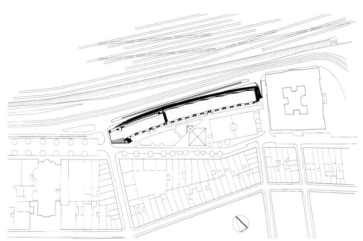

the stretched curvilinear building shields an intimate playground plaza from the busy, noisy infrastructure

On the other side, oriented to the south, are the balconies of the flats. For better light penetration and sightlines, they are positioned on a great concrete grid, which makes for greater privacy for the residents. It makes it difficult to look into the neighbours' balcony. For the passers-by in the street and in the plaza, the screen reinforces the individuality of the dwellings. A parking garage is located under the building.

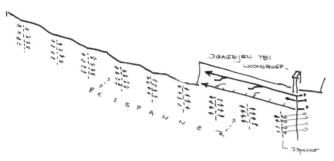

access principle: 9 stairwell foyers, and above this, galleries running from the end

glass screens in front of the galleries and balconies keep out traffic noise

2nd, 3rd, 4th floors

1st floor

ground floor of high-rise

stairwell foyer with various dwelling types

concrete screens on the plaza side of the building frame the balconies and provide privacy for the residents. the two balconies positioned one above the other do not take up the entire width of the flat, and are staggered so as to take away as little natural light from the lower flat as possible

the building stands on a narrow strip on the edge of the historic city centre, before the former harbour front, on a busy traffic artery with automobiles and trains

patio dwellings
9 dwellings (template)
1,000 m² GFA
1.0 FSi $_{net\ parcel}$
0.6 FSi $_{tissue}$
0.7 GSi $_{net\ parcel}$
0.4 GSi $_{tissue}$
stacking factor 1.5

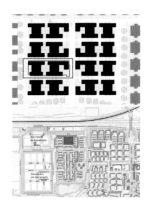

patio dwellings **geuzenveld**
amsterdam geuzenveld-slotermeer, 1988-1991
introvert residential environment, patio types
60 dwellings\hectare
narrow streets, 4 dwellings around 1 courtyard
cars out of the streetscape

In the early 1990s, a field of patio construction
was built in this expansion district of Amsterdam,
at a density of 60 dwellings per hectare. The area
has become available because the sports fields
that used to be there were moved further out of
town. Using narrow streets, an introvert residential
environment was created, with four dwellings
around one courtyard. It was not financially
feasible to give each dwelling its own patio.
We designed two types of patio dwellings, linked
so as to provide significant privacy. It is not easy
for residents to see inside one another's homes
from the courtyard. Varying the position of the
protrusions on the upper storey created variety
in the streetscape, which is dominated by the
long, high, blank (garden) walls with front doors.
Every few metres a structure protrudes above the
wall. The cars have vanished from the streets and
are parked in carports along the courtyards.
In the Netherlands, it is difficult to build patio
dwellings, because construction using concrete
poured in tunnel moulds is most cost-effective
for housing construction. The linked pattern in
Geuzenveld was made possible by simply building
the dwellings out of brick.

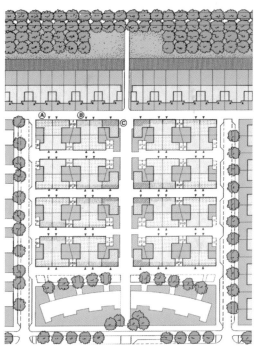

site

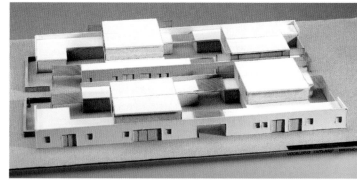

model of two templates

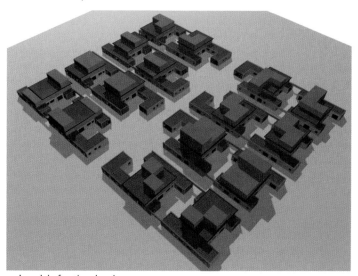

3-d model of entire planning area

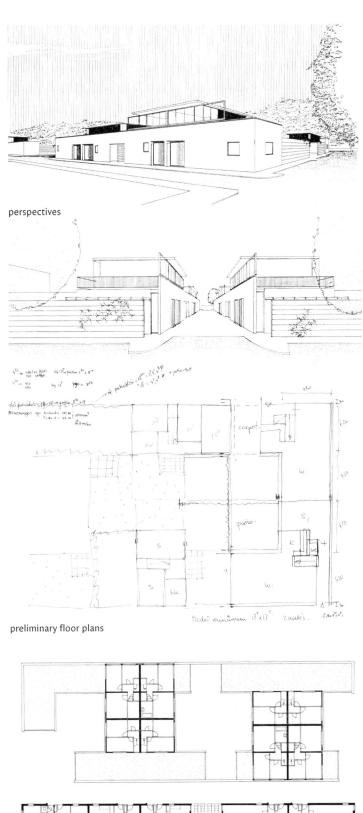

perspectives

preliminary floor plans

definitive floor plans for ground floor and upper floor

top to bottom: street, courtyard and courtyard access with carport

carré type building block
10 dwellings (template)
1,568 m² GFA
1.4 FSi net parcel
0.8 FSi tissue
0.7 GSi net parcel
0.4 GSi tissue
stacking factor 2.1

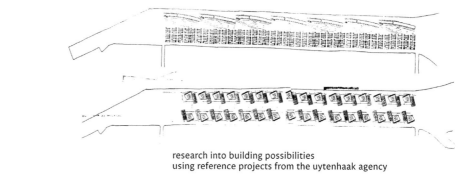

research into building possibilities
using reference projects from the uytenhaak agency

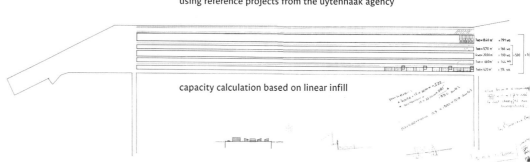

capacity calculation based on linear infill

java island study project
amsterdam, 1991
ground-linked dwellings per lateral metre
100 dwellings\hectare
dwelling type catalogue:
4-room duplex 95-115 m²
3-room flat (3 flats per storey) 81-103 m²
square 68-93 m²
star flat 78-87 m²
canal flat 80 m²
2-room garden flat 75 m²

Java Island is the first of a series of harbour islands
in the IJ in Amsterdam where new housing would
be built. Space had been made available by the
relocation of harbour activities. This plan is the
result of a study project into possibilities.
Our premise was to build high-density low-rise
housing, not to add more flats to Amsterdam's
housing stock. The quantity of dwellings
was particularly prescriptive for the design.
Every sketch bears capacity calculations in the
margin. In order to get a sense of the scale we
started drawing in our own reference projects.
The final design features a 5-storey rampart on the
north side, with flats favourably oriented toward
the south. They look out over the old city centre.
In front of these stands smaller-scale construction,
with ground-linked homes arranged around
courtyards. These dwellings are meant to offer an
alternative close to Amsterdam's city centre for
young families who had deserted the city. The city
employed this strategy on Borneo-Sporenburg.

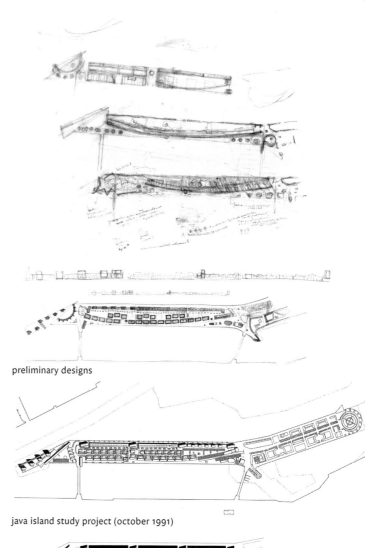

preliminary designs

java island study project (october 1991)

construction proposal

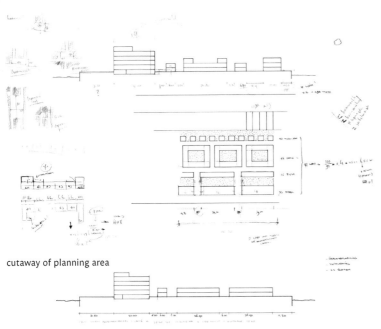

cutaway of planning area

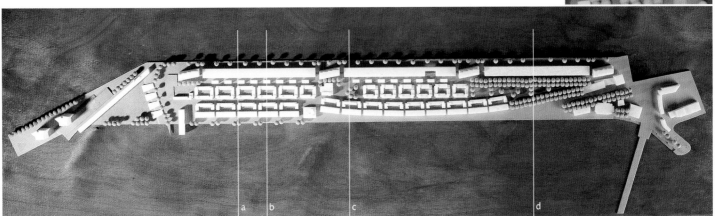

model of the construction proposal

north elevation

profiles a, b, c, d

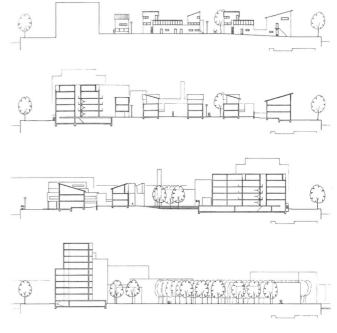

northwest elevation

slat dwellings
7 dwellings (template)
700 m² GFA
2.0 FSi net parcel
1.6 FSi gross parcel
0.7 GSi net parcel
0.5 GSi gross parcel
stacking factor 3.1

urban-design sketches

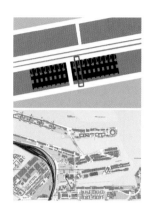

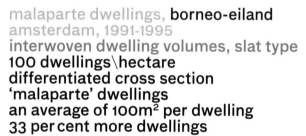

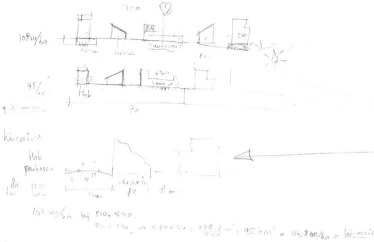

first concept: low-rise homes on gross parcels of 7×14 m

floor plan of ground floor and upper storey

malaparte dwellings, **borneo-eiland**
amsterdam, 1991-1995
interwoven dwelling volumes, slat type
100 dwellings\hectare
differentiated cross section
'malaparte' dwellings
an average of 100m² per dwelling
33 per cent more dwellings

The first dwelling concept shows that with a parcel allotment into gross parcels of 7×14 m, a density of 100 dwellings per hectare is feasible. A series of other typologies elaborated into an urban-design sketch for Sporenburg extends the range. Six different architects came up with building blocks for this structure, whereupon a competition for the urban-design plan was launched. West 8 won this competition. To vouchsafe the feasibility of this design, we were subsequently asked to develop a dwelling catalogue for the elaboration of the 'slats' in this plan. Later still in the process, a shortage of ground-linked and publicly subsidized rental dwellings threatened to emerge. We then proposed a three-dimensional interweaving of seven dwellings per module of 8.4×43 m. Angled roofs, terraces and patios provide the necessary privacy to the individual dwellings. This resulted in a 33 per cent increase in density. Every dwelling has a front door on the street and a living room that looks out onto the street, and is therefore connected with the city. This panoramic view also ensures that residents do not feel too constricted in this dense urban tissue.

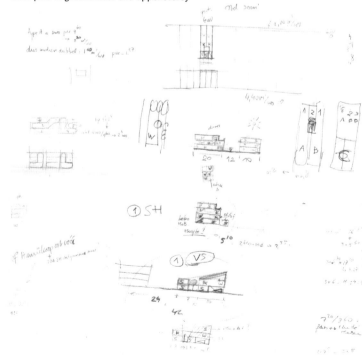

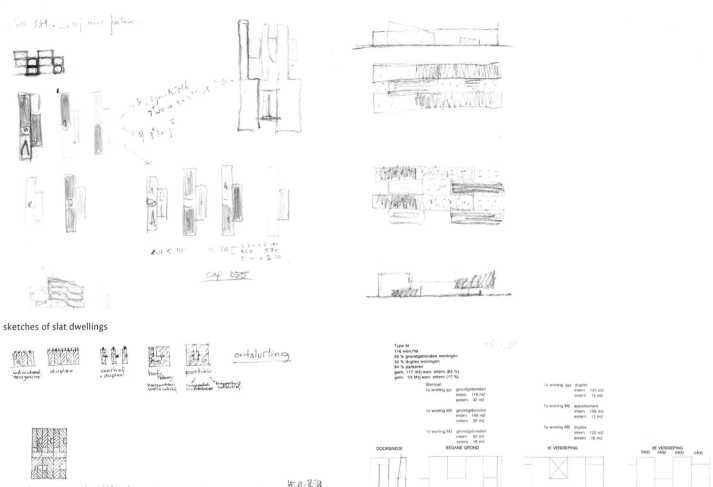

sketches of slat dwellings

floor plans studies for back-to-back patio slat dwellings

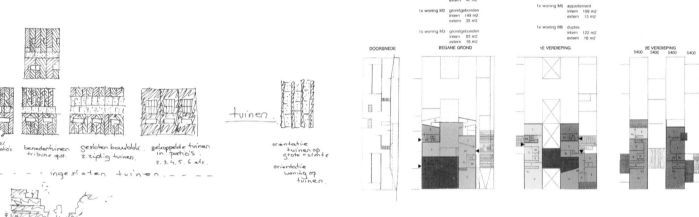

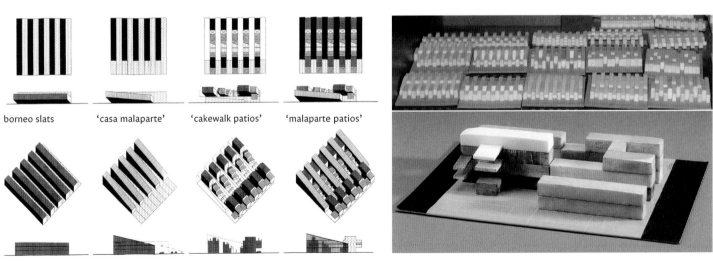

borneo slats   'casa malaparte'   'cakewalk patios'   'malaparte patios'

second concept, over the entire parcel depth. combining variants 2 and 3 produces variant 4: long building blocks with patios interspersed with patios

malaparte cross sections and floor plans showing interconnected templates, each consisting of 7 dwellings.

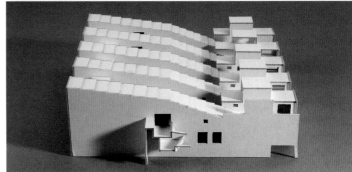

models

bird's-eye view

north façade, feike de boerlaan

stepped courtyard to the southeast, with balconies and two patios

south façade on the borneokade

villas, 2, 3, 4 and 8 semi-detached
ground-connected dwellings
and maisonnettes
52 dwellings (template)
6,845 m² GFA
1.5 FSi net parcel*
1.0 FSi tissue
0.5 GSi net parcel
0.3 GSi tissue
stacking factor 3.2

*FSi measured for a representative template at
the tissue level

at an early design stage, some of
the parking facilities were clustered
under the green zones

premises for the design

instead of terraced house: villa

instead of public gardens: private gardens

cars not on the street: on private property

instead of sorting: mixing

instead of a village green: a city window

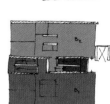

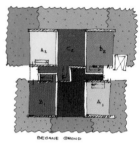

six semi-detached dwellings:
each dwelling has its own garden
and a garden room on the ground
floor. access by internal stairs and
perhaps a lift

de bongerd dwellings
amsterdam-noord, 1994-2005
garden suburb revisited in high density
an average of 70 dwellings\hectare
arrangements of 2 to 8 semi-detached dwellings
1,640 dwellings

De Bongerd is actually a high-density garden
suburb, in other words a garden city. As a result
it fits in with the characteristic garden suburbs of
Amsterdam-Noord. It is urban in its programme,
but not in its appearance. Residential buildings
varying from two to eight semi-detached dwellings
and urban villas form an extensive field of small
building volumes surrounded by private gardens.
The different residential buildings are mixed
together, as it were, creating a rich variety in the
streetscape. The mixture has been composed
using a spreadsheet: more of one automatically
led to less of the other. Cars are parked on private
property and are therefore less dominant in the
streetscape. In the two to eight semi-detached
dwelling combinations, each dwelling has at least
one room that overlooks the garden. And every
garden room has its own garden.

models of the block types

TWEEONDEREENKAP
62.5wo/hA

DRIEONDEREENKAP
71.43wo/hA

VIERONDEREENKAP
93.02wo/hA

ZESONDEREENKAP
95.24wo/hA

ACHTONDEREENKAP
108.10wo/hA

URBAN VILLA'S
100wo/hA

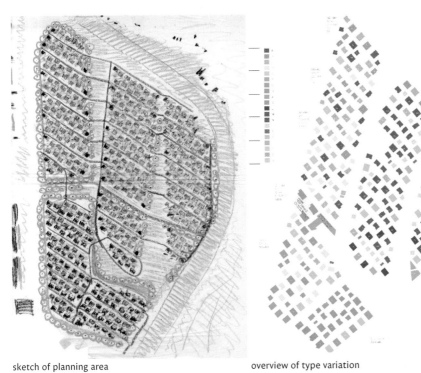
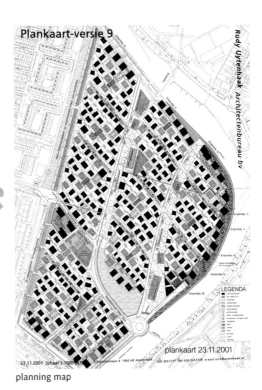

sketch of planning area

overview of type variation

planning map

Plankaart-versie 9

plankaart 23.11.2001

Rudy Uytenhaak Architectenbureau bv

LEGENDA

mixture represented by liquorice all-sorts and calculated using the spreadsheet

spreadsheet dwelling differentiation used to assess land occupancy and number of dwellings

Bongerd - WONINGDIFFERENTIATIE - d.d. 27 september 2002

TOETSING GRONDBESLAG EN WONINGAANTAL PER WOONGEBIED

WOONGEBIED	1-kap	2-kap	3-kap-1	3-kap-2	4-VS	6-VE	6-VS/g	6-SH	7-VS	8-VE	8-SH	stadsvilla	Tuin	PT	deurzet	woningen	grondbeslag
Woongebied A	3	50	33	9	72	42	18	36	0	0	80	60	0	3	4	403	43355
%totaal/type	1%	36%	13%	3%	21%	4%	50%	21%	#DEEL/0!	0%	29%	14%	0%	21%	27%		
Woongebied G	4	12	3	3	8	0	0	0	0	0	0	0	0	2	0	30	4812
%totaal/type	25%	9%	7%	3%	3%	0%	0%	0%	#DEEL/0!	0%	0%	0%	0%	0%			
Woongebied B	1	18	3	15	56	18	6	30	0	8	40	23	0	2	3	218	27837
%totaal/type	6%	13%	7%	15%	21%	18%	17%	17%	#DEEL/0!	25%	15%	6%	0%	15%	20%		
Woongebied C	0	0	0	0	0	0	0	0	0	0	0	25	0	0	0	25	1500
%totaal/type	0%	0%	0%	0%	0%	0%	0%	0%	#DEEL/0!	0%	0%	6%	0%	0%			
Woongebied D	4	36	6	33	84	24	12	60	0	16	72	79	0	3	2	426	42769
%totaal/type	25%	26%	13%	33%	32%	24%	33%	34%	#DEEL/0!	50%	26%	19%	0%	21%	13%		
Woongebied E	1	10	0	15	12	0	0	18	0	0	32	71	1	1	0	180	14395
%totaal/type	6%	7%	0%	15%	5%	0%	0%	10%	#DEEL/0!	0%	12%	1%	100%	9%	7%		
Woongebied F	3	14	0	24	32	18	0	30	0	8	48	159	0	2	3	336	28550
%totaal/type	19%	10%	0%	24%	12%	18%	0%	17%	#DEEL/0!	25%	19%	38%	0%	15%	20%		

TOTAAL																woningen	grondbeslag
Ruimtebeslag	210	330	420	420	470	560	560	520	600	610	570	60	50	225	360		163218
Aantal blokken	16	70	15	33	66	17	6	29	0	4	34	417	21	11	15		
Aantal woningen	16	140	45	99	264	102	36	174	0	32	272	417	21			**1618 woninge**	
	3360	23100	6300	8360	31020	9520	3360	19080	0	2440	9280	25020	1050	2475	5400	7546	
Sociale huur	0	0		0	0	0	0	174	0	0	272	0	21			**467**	28,86%
Vrije sector	16	140		99	264	102	36	0	0	32	0	417	0			**1106**	68,36%

Straatparkeren	PT	straat		wig	bezoek	TOTAAL	excl.PT		Prive-parkeren			1135		Parkeergarages	
Aanbod	176	250		34	162	622	448		Erf		831	0,51	pp/wo	Ensembles	
Vraag	176		272		162	610	434		Drive-in		222	0,14	pp/wo	P-7 voor 7-kap	
NB Het aanbod overtreft de vraag: MARGE!									Carport		82	0,05	pp/wo	P-7 voor anderen	

Woningtype	1-kap	2-kap	3-kap	3-kap	4-kap	6-kap	6-cp	6-kap	7-kap	8-kap	8-kap	stadsvilla	stadsvilla	Tuin			
en ruimtebeslag*	210	330	420	420	470	560	560	520	600	610	570	60	50	225	360		
Ruimtebeslag is indicatief	200	320	420	420	465	560	560	510	585	610	570	60	46	200			6260

WOONGEBIED A	1-kap	2-kap	3-kap	3-kap	4-VS	6-VE	6-VS/g	6-SH	7-VS	8-VE	8-SH	stadsvilla	Tuin	PT	deurzet	woningen	grondbeslag
A1	0	1	2	0	0	1	0	0	0	0	1	80	0	0	1	02	6260

detached house, 210 m² parcel   2 semi-detached, 330 m² parcel   3 semi-detached, 420 m² parcel   4 semi-detached, 470 m² parcel   6 semi-det. + carport, 560 m² parcel

1 dwelling, 160 m² usable surface
2 cars on property
1 storage space

2 dwellings, 152-155 m² usable s.
2 cars in drive-in garage and
2 on property, 2 storage spaces.
variant: living space on ground
floor instead of drive-in garage

3 dwellings, 130 m² usable s.
2 drive-in parking spaces,
3 on property, 3 storage spaces.
variant: no drive-in facility

4 dwellings, 120 m² usable s.
4 cars on property and 2 on
the street, 4 storage spaces

6 private sector dwellings, 113 m² u.
4 carports, 3 cars on the street
6 storage spaces, collective front
garden, 5 gardens and 3 roof terrace

general view of planning area

cutaway with the arrangement of two templates

6 semi-detached in quadrant, 520 m² parcel

7 semi-detached dwellings, 585 m² parcel

8 semi-detached with 8 gardens, 610 m² parcel

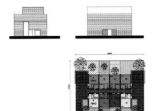

6 dwellings in villa building, 110 m² usable s.
4 cars on property, 3 on the street
6 storage spaces with street access
4 gardens and 2 roof terraces
collective courtyard, tree, bike storage
all dwellings diagonal. 4 maisonettes with
garden, 2 penthouses of 147 m²

7 publicly subsidized rental dwellings, 107 m² us.
14 cars in garage, 14 on access incline
7 ground level storage spaces
7 gardens and 6 roof terraces
naturally ventilated parking garage

8 dwellings, 90 m² usable surface
4 cars on property, 4 on the street
8 storage spaces, entrance alley with natural light.
a garden room for every dwelling. maisonettes
with garden or garden and roof terrace

de bongerd garden city shortly after completion. the vegetation still has to reach full growth

apartments,
work-at-home dwellings
296 dwellings (template)
(incl. commercial space,
day-care centre, etc.)
52,069 m² GFA
3.8 FSi net parcel
1.9 FSi tissue
0.6 GSi net parcel
0.3 GSi tissue
stacking factor 6.4

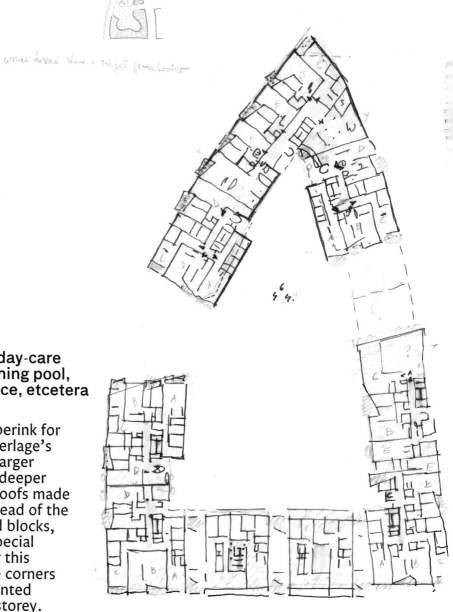

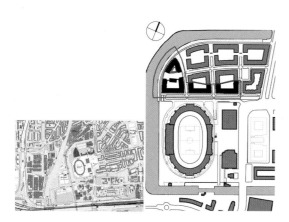

olympisch kwartier dwellings
amsterdam-zuid, 1999-2004
maximized perimeter block

296 dwellings, commercial space, day-care centre, communal facilities, swimming pool, fitness facility, resident's hotel, office, etcetera
7 per cent more dwellings

The urban design by Lafour, Wijk & Ebberink for this site represents a continuation of Berlage's Plan Zuid, but with larger dwellings in larger blocks. In addition, making the blocks deeper and using the space under the angled roofs made it possible to realize 296 dwellings instead of the 277 that had been requested. In closed blocks, the dwellings at the corners demand special attention in terms of sun exposure. For this reason, there are three dwellings in the corners on the east side, while the corners oriented to the west feature four dwellings per storey. The dwellings on the west side get afternoon sun and have a view of the Stadiongracht.
The idea was for the buildings to fit in with the Amsterdam School style of Zuid. This entailed closed brick façades with relatively small windows. In order to provide the dwellings with great views and natural light, the brickwork was positioned like pennants in front of the window frames. The formal character of the building is maintained by giving the dwellings on the Stadionweg a conservatory at the front and a balcony on the garden side. The large, tapered residential block is outfitted with communal facilities, such as a swimming pool, a fitness facility, meeting rooms and extra guest quarters.

view onto the historic stadium and onto the stadiongracht

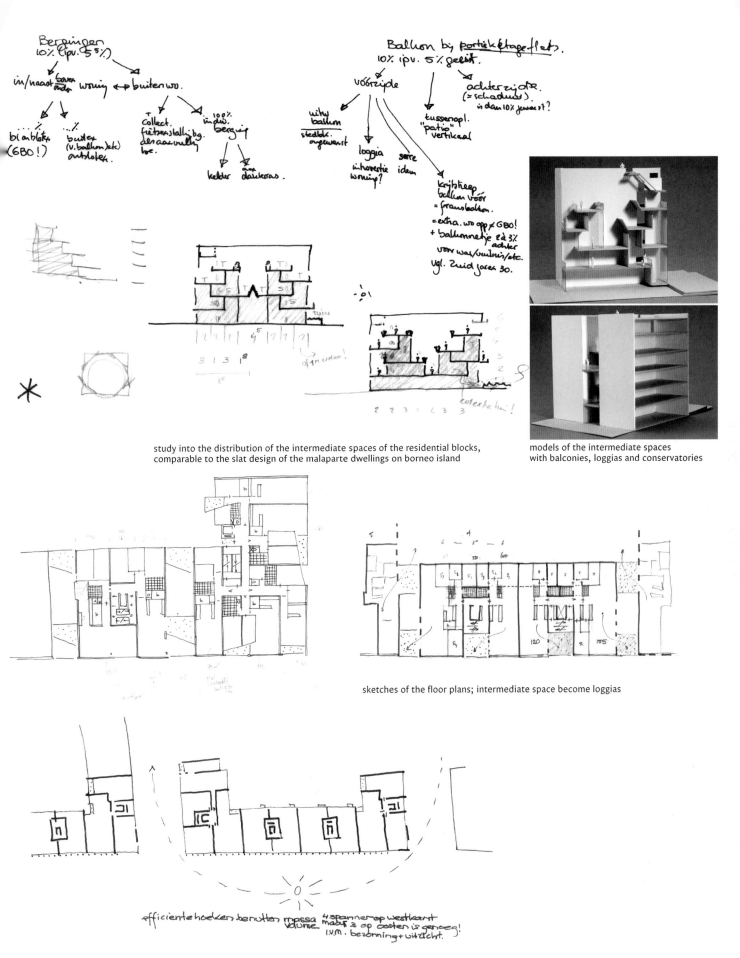

study into the distribution of the intermediate spaces of the residential blocks, comparable to the slat design of the malaparte dwellings on borneo island

models of the intermediate spaces with balconies, loggias and conservatories

sketches of the floor plans; intermediate space become loggias

sketch of sun exposure: 3 dwellings at the east corner, 4 dwellings at the west corner, because these have better sun exposure and better views

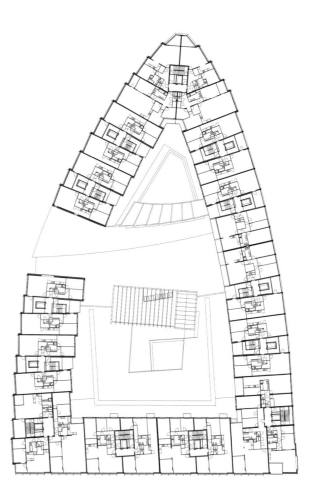

brick pennants positioned in front of the window frames

elevation from the northwest, with the stadiongracht in the centre and the schinkel in the foreground

view through to the inner courtyard of the tapered block

a few floor plans of dwellings in the tapered block

apartments, maisonettes
and terraced houses
179 dwellings (template)
(incl. commercial space)
23,283 m² GFA
2.3 FSi net parcel*
1.4 FSi tissue
0.8 GSi net parcel
0.5 GSi tissue
stacking factor 3

*FSi measured for the ensemble (not per type)

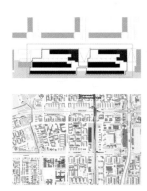

veltmanstraat residential buildings
amsterdam slotervaart, 1999-2003
optimal dwelling number, types and orientation
uptown\downtown
instead of 120 apartments 179 dwellings (including 70 single-family homes) were realized, as well as commercial spaces 35 per cent more than prescribed by the urban-design schedule of requirements

The urban design proposed four urban villas on the site of a former school. To avoid these dwellings ending up on ground-level site dominated by a car park, greater density was proposed, so that a parking garage could be funded. In addition, this would result in a richer differentiation among dwelling typologies. Hook-shaped apartment buildings, decreasing in height toward the south to allow for large terraces, rest on a base of maisonettes. Above these are apartments accessed by a lift. The single-family homes behind the block of flats sit on the roof of the sunken parking garage. The second row of homes is at ground level and borders the water. The low-rise dwellings that have a patio or a garden are accessed by an internal corridor. The public spaces between the blocks fit in with Van Eesteren's strip parcel allotment in the adjacent neighbourhood.

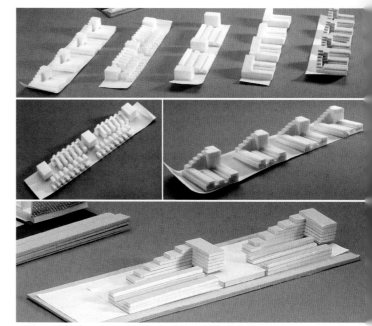

study models: from tower blocks via slats to 2 blocks and 4 strips

a stepped block and two strips of single-family homes per template

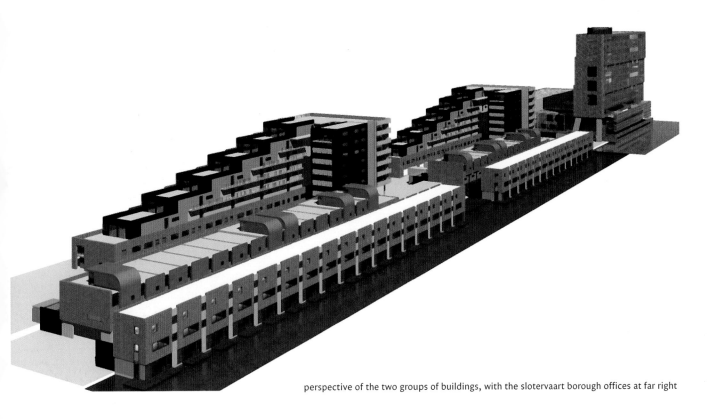

perspective of the two groups of buildings, with the slotervaart borough offices at far right

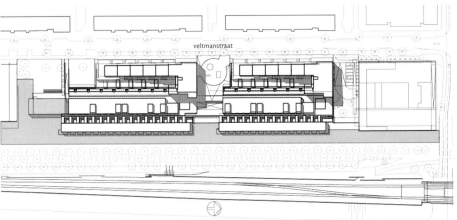

veltmanstraat

general map, with the railroad embankment in the foreground. a public garden connects the templates

south façade elevation with cross section of the parking garage

veltmanstraat façade elevation

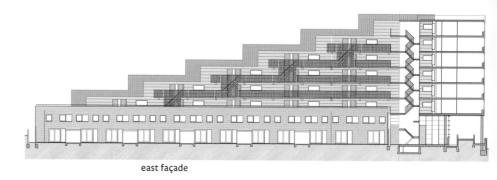

east façade

east façade of the strip of dwellings on top of the parking garage

end façade and east façade of the strip of dwellings on the water

ground-linked dwellings in the residential high-rise

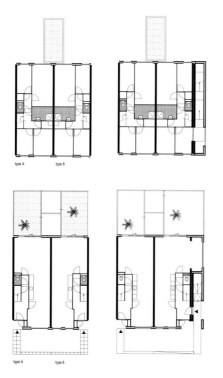

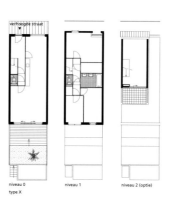

floor plans of the dwellings above the parking garage

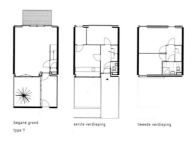

floor plans of the dwellings on the water

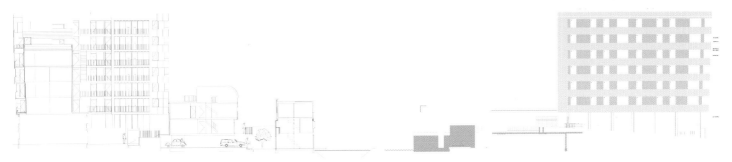

diagonal cross section across the whole with parking garage.
the curved arrangement of the strip in the middle is an option

north side end façades

interior area

veltmanstraat elevation

on the left, the dwellings above the parking garage

dwellings on the water

apartments
115 dwellings
(incl. health center, etc.)
25,446 m² GFA
12.6 FSi net parcel
4.9 FSi tissue
1.0 GSi net parcel
0.4 GSi tissue
stacking factor 12.6

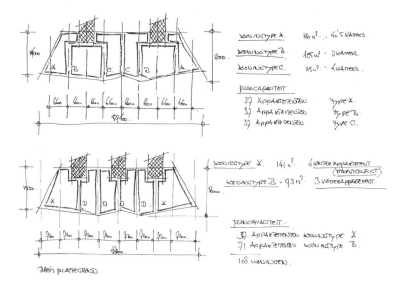

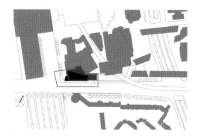

preliminary studies with 2 or 3 stairwells for every 6 dwellings. in the end, 2 stairwells serve 7 dwellings (one side with 4 and one side with 3 dwellings) per residential storey

la fenêtre residential building
the hague city centre, 1994-2006
maximum floor space index

115 dwellings and 150 cars, as well as a new pedestrian area on a site where 20 cars used to be parked: three hectares less urban expansion! creating space in the existing city

An out-of-the-way leftover space in the angle formed by the Prins Bernhard viaduct and The Hague Central bus station used to provide parking for 20 cars. Now the site houses 115 dwellings, 150 parking spaces and a new pedestrian area. The residential building sits atop tall, slender steel columns and has 17 storeys. It was initially to be built in the vicinity of the Utrechtsebaan, but noise regulations for 70-kph roadways meant that the structure had to be shifted some distance away. The building is actually a fusion of two blocks of flats with lobbies that face each other. In one, dwellings are arranged in groups of four around the lift shaft, while in the other there are three dwellings per storey. The building is widest toward the southwest, in order to take optimal advantage of sun exposure and the view of the city. A parking garage has been accommodated in the base of the structure.

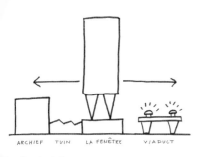

project logistics

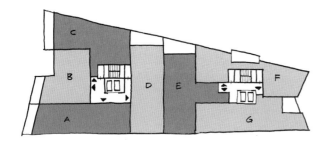

final dwelling distribution per residential storey

entrance to lobby with the flats high above, lifted above the city

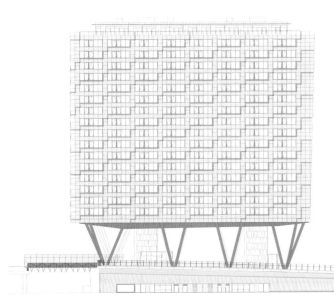

side façade and end façade elevation

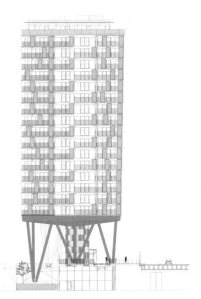

parking in the base, with the pedestrian area above, at the level of the viaduct

apartements
28 dwellings (template)
16,436 m² GFA
(incl. commercial space)
4.8 FSi net parcel
3.0 FSi tissue
1.0 GSi net parcel
0.6 GSi tissue
stacking factor 4.9

existing plan

apartements
70 dwellings (template)
19,156 m² GFA
(incl. commercial space)
5.6 FSi net parcel
3.5 FSi tissue
1.0 GSi net parcel
0.6 GSi tissue
stacking factor 5.6

modified plan

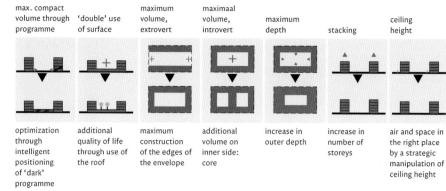

max. compact volume through programme	'double' use of surface	maximum volume, extrovert	maximaal volume, introvert	maximum depth	stacking	ceiling height
optimization through intelligent positioning of 'dark' programme	additional quality of life through use of the roof	maximum construction of the edges of the envelope	additional volume on inner side: core	increase in outer depth	increase in number of storeys	air and space in the right place by a strategic manipulation of ceiling height

7 options for increasing capacity within the urban-design envelope

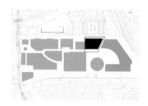

study project, **dwellings and dance studio**
amsterdam, 2008
optimum block capacity

The study represents a search for the maximum capacity for the site in Amsterdam-Oost. How many dwellings can be realized on this site, without negatively affecting the quality of the individual dwellings? The parcel combines dwellings with a dance studio, parking, a café/restaurant and commercial spaces. An earlier plan for the same site, not designed by Uytenhaak, serves as a reference model. The capacity of the plan has been increased by making the base of the building one storey higher and using this storey to house the programme for which natural light is not needed. The storeys above this have been changed from two separate strips into one block. A central and wider courtyard ensures sufficient natural light. Placing the traffic areas on the inside allows the dwellings to benefit from the maximum length of the façade on the outside of the block. The courtyard becomes smaller at the location of the dance studio, while it is larger alongside the dwellings; the building volume makes use of the difference in natural light requirements. In several stages, the housing programme has grown from 28 gallery dwellings to 70 dwellings in seven- and eight-flat arrangement per storey. These floor-lobby dwellings, with either seven or eight flats per vertical access, offer more compactness and privacy that dwellings along a gallery. Giving the dwellings greater ceiling heights, at the cost of one storey, makes them more spacious and better lit, and still results in 55 dwellings, 27 more than the reference model.

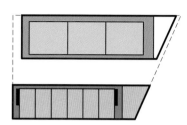

levels 2-5

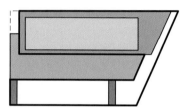

level 1

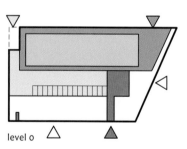

level 0

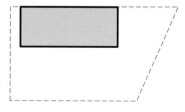

level -1

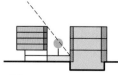

reference model:
schematic specification of storeys and cross section
4 storeys of 7 gallery flats = 28 dwellings
plus required square footage for dance studio

4 storeys of 10 flats each = 40 flats

step 2

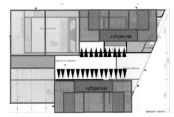

4 storeys of 10 flats each (2 x 5 flats) = 40 flats

step 3

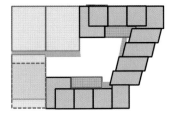

4 storeys of 14 flats each = 56 flats

step 4

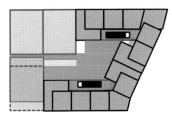

4 storeys of 15 flats each = 60 flats (see upper right)

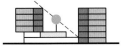

or

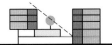

fewer flats: 3 storeys of 15 flats each = 45
results in greater ceiling height, space and light penetration

optimization through intelligent positioning of 'dark' programme

maximum construction of the edges of the envelope

additional volume on inner side: core

increase in capacity in the case of the project involving flats + dance studio

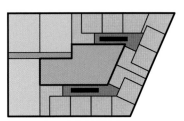

floors 2-5:
4 storeys of 15 flats each = 60 flats

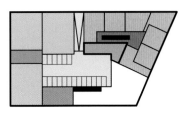

first floor:
dance studio, 7 flats, café/restaurant
29 parking places

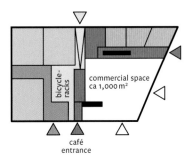

ground floor:
dance studio, 3 flats
commercial space, about 1,000 m²
bicycle racks, storage, access to parking garage,
entrance to café\restaurant

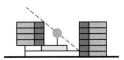

the modified design accommodates:
in total, 60 + 3 + 7 = 70 flats
a dance studio, in keeping with the programme
commercial space, about 1,000 m² and café\restaurant
29 parking places, bicycle racks,
storage spaces, patio

spatial quality: compensation for density

proximity is the key to the city's appeal. being close to others increases opportunities for communication, trade, cooperation, influence. this wealth in the form of variety in and of proximity is one reason why many people want to live in densely built cities. cities are where it's happening! to many, being able to take part in this urban diversity at individual levels in Maslow's hierarchy of needs – let's call them physical, consumptive, sensual and mental – represents the freedom of the city.

There are other – obvious – advantages to densely built cities. They take up less space, land and infrastructure (streets, mains, lighting, and so forth) and require less maintenance. The unoccupied space remains available for other activities, for landscape, other sources of existence or expansion. **density, however, also has a menacing, claustrophobic effect. it generates sensory stress.** People need their own world and privacy. This is why distance is imperative in a city. It provides distinction to develop individual activities. Distance provides independence, which one must also be able to maintain, however. If this is possible, it provides status and perhaps results in less vulnerability.

sydney, rio de janeiro

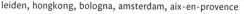

leiden, hongkong, bologna, amsterdam, aix-en-provence

9
rudy uytenhaak, inaugural address *ruimte dichten. opdracht, visie en passie* eindhoven university of technology, faculty of architecture 1991.

Legally mandated distances between buildings are partly determined by natural light requirements. They are simply expressed by the angle of obstruction. Too simply.

privacy should involve a balance between showing yourself and hiding yourself. the architect mediates between city and intimacy. he creates neither – perhaps the space in between.[9]

Architecture is the intermediary for creating the potential to establish contact with and the potential to shield yourself from others. This can be achieved with little details, so that you can filter things, flip switches. Distance is created by spreading out. In a spatial sense, in fabrics and patterns, dilution creates space between the building blocks. In a literal sense, this space provides air and visibility, light, transparency, but this space also makes it possible to integrate new functions into the city. Automobile traffic can be accommodated by one existing urban tissue (for instance the Eixample in Barcelona) but not by another (the historic city centre). Spreading not only provides space for concrete functions, but also for interpretations and temporary activities and experiments, for example.

space makes the city legible

Excessive compression not only reduces the physical transparency of visibility and light, but compression without scale also reduces orientation. It makes it impossible to provide, within the visual perspective or during a stroll, different vistas that not only make the city more varied and interesting, but also provide insight into the city as a whole. This is an important spatial quality, which we identify with the criterion of 'scale' and which stands for the experience of coherence and diversity. For scale refers to the proportion between details and the whole, in terms both of quantity and of character. A powerful or simple whole with lively or rich details, for instance, or the other way round.

detail and whole tell each other about large and small, light and dark, simplicity and complexity.

Every time, this creates individual identities featuring that unique balance of dynamism and familiar stability (comfort, style, perfection).

for orientation, this perception of space is dominant.

Especially when the space, or perhaps a building, as a container of events, carries meaning and is identifiable, or even has a name. Such as a familiar square or an impressive building.

These nameable identities are necessary to find one's way in the city or to explain it to others. If the city is too easily memorable and legible, it is dull. Those moving about the city look for continuity and variety – certainly when they regularly follow the same route. Variations in types of buildings, varying street profiles, squares and unique buildings ensure that the route through the urban tissue remains an interesting experience. It is a form of staging of the view in the space of urban design. This means buildings must be positioned so as to create varying perspectives. For the necessary openness at ground level, there are rivers, parks, boulevards and squares. Superimposing different networks produces greater topographic recognizability in the city.

so there must be a balance between legibility and variety, reassurance and stimulation, order and surprise. this requires an urban design strategy.

new york, pompidou plage, maastricht, gouda, bordeaux, amsterdam

eixample, barcelona

rational grid versus mediaeval city: cerdà versus sitte

In the history of urban design, two outlooks can be distinguished, which represent the two ends of a spectrum. On the one hand are the proponents of the grid city. They point to Milete or perhaps to Ildefons Cerdà's urban design plan for the Eixample in Barcelona. In a neutral grid, each block is independent and can develop in a unique way. Rationality and optimization of the basic structure are given priority, but at the same time this structure has a beauty all its own.

On the other hand there is the organic medieval city as a shining example, as promoted by Camillo Sitte. This approach allows variety in all aspects, such as scale, grain, dynamism of space and mass.

it is instructive to know how much difference you need to evoke the perception of rich variety.

For the urban plan of the Bongerd development in Amsterdam we ranked liquorice all-sorts. We discovered that just a few different types of liquorice produce a sense of variety that cannot be immediately summed up. And this is only a simple mixture. The city is made up of many more ingredients.

Another strategy is to achieve variety with entirely identical sugar cubes, but then by introducing different dimensions among the blocks.

It is a question of varying space, not of differing masses. The Passeig de Gracia in Barcelona, designed by Cerdà, is one example of this. The profile and ornamentation of the urban design is more important than its structure. All the blocks in the grid, after all, are identical in size. Compare this with Loos's view of architecture: 'The walls are what you perceive.'

The question remains whether we achieve abundance by introducing variety in the space or in the mass. Orientation is a compelling consideration in making that choice. One strategy might work better than another for projects of a certain scale and for certain locations. In a small village, there are fixed points, such as the church or the square. In a Dutch Vinex housing development or other forms of urban sprawl, or in a kasbah, where the expression of the individual blocks has essentially been negated, the interstitial space has more significance than the mass.

In the Novartis district in Basel by Lampugnani, many aspects come together. The plan uses different street profiles, different moments, long streets, short streets, some bordering a square. It is a very abundant plan, made up of simple elements. This plan combines the qualities of Sitte and Cerdà.

aix-en-provence

novartis quarter, basel

orientation

I believe in the Loos principle, which says that the ornamentation of public space, through function, paving, façades and trees, is dominant. And I believe that Sitte's outlook is architecturally romantic, nestled in complexity. As the scale of the area increases, however, a need for transparency arises. However exciting it might be to wander around such 'Sitte neighbourhoods', you need places where you can orient yourself. There need to be structures that make it clear how the city is constructed. This is one of the reasons why, in Paris and Rome, structures are still being added to fit the new scale of these cities. These interventions form an intermediary between the scale of the whole city and that of the smaller island. Inside these islands, a more intricate, Sitte-like structure can be created. In reality this was also, in part, H.P. Berlage's strategy for Plan Zuid in Amsterdam. In addition to the great thoroughfares, with smaller axes perpendicular to them, he sometimes made groups of housing blocks you can get lost in. Cornelis van Eesteren, with his dwellings arranged around courtyards in the Westelijke Tuinsteden, actually did not differ all that much from Berlage. In terms of the use of scale, they are comparable. Berlage and Van Eesteren were both looking for a stepping stone into the city. Once a certain scale is reached, this is a necessary marker on which to base a mental map of the city. Within this map, one zooms in on the various islands. The difference between the two is that one made routes and the other made fields. Berlage made combinations of closed housing blocks and Van Eesteren made templates of tower blocks. If we compare Buitenveldert, a garden-city district in the south of Amsterdam and a later design by Van Eesteren, with the rich variety of Berlage's Plan Zuid (an 1914 urban design for the south side of Amsterdam), let alone with the city centre of Utrecht, we notice that Buitenveldert can be quickly summed up in terms of cartography and ingredients. The recipe of using a few variations in simple zones seems insufficient after all.

it is therefore crucial to create a series of variations in the breadth and height of the street and of the buildings, as well as different colours. these, applied in alternation or at random, produce more potential variety and therefore abundance.

privacy in dwelling access

Even buildings themselves should provide compensation for density to their users. The dwelling will have to be spacious. At higher densities, the space required for a function, the space it takes up, increases. A lack of 'runback space' creates a need for relaxation. In the home, this need can be satisfied in square and cubic metres. A living room or study looking out onto a garden, after all, has a different spatial effect than that of a comparable room high up in the air.

the dwelling must also create some emotional distance from the density of the city.

The city provides room to meet people, but certainly to avoid them, as well. There are choices. The urban dweller is Walter Benjamin's flâneur. In a residential building, this freedom is far more curtailed. Residents are more directly connected to one another. This can be oppressive, especially if different subcultures have to use the common route in different ways and at different times. On the street this is generally accepted and even seen as a typically enriching aspect of city life. In a residential building, however, the concentrated nature of access quickly leads to irritation.

in order to reduce the likelihood of unwanted encounters and mutual irritations as much as possible, we keep the semi-public route in our buildings as short as possible.

Herman Hertzberger and Le Corbusier, on the contrary, encouraged mutual encounters in their residential buildings. In essence

they were creating commune buildings rather than urban residential buildings. In their designs the residential building and its facilities replaced the city. Such an approach, while romantically appealing, can only work if the target populations are precisely defined and more or less related to one another.

If the target populations are divergent, collectivity has to be designed out of a complex, the way we did it in the residential complex Hoop, Liefde en Fortuin in Amsterdam. Here, elderly residents are housed in the same complex as relatively large families and starter residents. You can well imagine that the habits of this collection of residents are too divergent for a functional, shared access. Therefore only the outer entrance is communal. From here each of the four dwellings is accessed by its own stairwell. Several functional preconditions made the floor plans more complex. For example, the living room had to be on the street side, and the bedrooms at the back. To prevent noise nuisance, living rooms are always positioned one on top of the other. All of this makes for a complex building floor plan; the floor plan of the dwellings themselves is relatively simple. As it happens, this 'complexity' is perceived as a plus by many residents. It has led to atypical and therefore almost individual dwelling floor plans. The fact that there are more stairs than in a standard residential building is seen as an acceptable side-effect. In addition to heightened privacy, designing out communal access also produces lower maintenance and management costs.

in taller buildings, this kind of private access is almost impossible. access from the central lobby is therefore the most direct route from the front door to the street. only the lift and the lobby are communal.

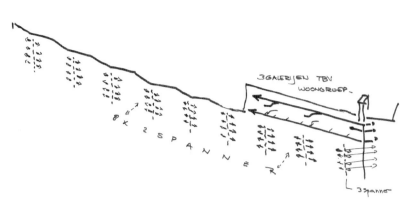

access programme of droogbak residential building

examples of internal galleries with voids

i avoid galleries wherever possible. they produce one-way routes that are too long. galleries are not spaces, but their cramped dimensions create too many ledges in a building.

There are very few galleries of any quality. Michiel Brinkman's Justus van Effen complex in the Spangen district of Rotterdam is one example. The gallery, along which the flats are ranged, is situated between two lobbies, so that residents can turn left or right onto the gallery. Furthermore, this gallery open to the sky features adequate dimensions, enabling people to pass one another discreetly and even creating an abode quality. The potential to 'walk around' increases the sense of freedom, and especially the sense of security. Bjarne Mastenbroek also designed a nice gallery in the Leidsche Rijn development in Utrecht. He used bridges to create a circuit. However, if there is no budget for more lifts, galleries are unavoidable. This was the case in the flats for elderly residents in Hoop, Liefde en Fortuin. By turning the gallery into a circuit and making it a bit deeper you can make it acceptable. Just adding nice decoration and details is too superficial. It might provide greater status, but in the long term residents are better served by spatial quality.

An entrance lobby can provide access for two, three or as many as eight dwellings. The more dwellings, the greater the percentage of unilaterally oriented floor plans. Interweaving the dwellings does create an even greater differentiation, but one wonders why we are so stingy on this point in the Netherlands and why we don't simply build double-sided structures that allow access from both sides of the building.

floor plan privacy
a sense of privacy is not just a matter of access. the floor plan of the dwelling is also crucial. especially how independent the dwelling is from that communal access.

With a gallery this is virtually impossible. The gallery compresses the link with the world and compromises the privacy of the dwelling. It is almost inevitable that bedrooms will be situated along the gallery, with people constantly walking by. This is unpleasant, and as a result residents turn away from the gallery. Curtains are drawn and remain closed.

With his galleries in Amsterdam-Noord, Frans van Gool provides access to three floors at a time. You use stairs to go up or down. With this he has increased the options for designing the floor plan. The living spaces no longer have to be situated directly along the semi-public space of the building. In effect he has modified the corridor access.

galleries linked by bridges, leidsche rijn

balconies as recesses in the building volume

The corridor also means that many rooms can be situated, unencumbered, along the façade. One big drawback is the often narrow, oppressive hallway in the heart of the building, reminiscent of a hotel or nursing home. Moreover, stairs to access the different dwellings are often necessary. Shifting the corridor to the façade at least removes the first drawback. As it happens, in Golden Lane in London the Smithsons also shifted the corridor, providing access to multiple floors, to the façade, as it were. Whether the corridor is situated along the façade or in the middle of the building, the way in which the individual dwellings are accessed is practically the same. The actual residential level is reached via a small private level.

Maisonettes along a gallery deliver the same advantages as a corridor. The vulnerable rooms are not situated along the gallery either. In this dwelling typology, however, the living room is usually at the level of the gallery. The private level remains separate, and visitors do not have to climb stairs.

genuinely interesting ways of providing access are created when the dwellings themselves feature multiple entrances and diverse routes (front and back, service routes, roof galleries) run through the building. this concept is seldom applied, however.

examples of balconies that provide shelter from the outside world

Creating privacy around the home can also be achieved with smaller details. When peeping is made visible, this heightens the sense of privacy. This plays a role in the placement of balconies in a collective residential building. Balconies positioned one on top of the other in a straight line deliver the most privacy. But balconies can also be staggered. This comes at the cost of privacy, but in spatial terms it is more interesting. The occupant gets more space above his or her balcony. Moreover, the balcony's natural light penetration is also improved. When balconies are positioned and constructed so that people have to lean out of their balconies to be able to spy on their neighbours, this magnifies social pressure to such a degree that the spying virtually ceases.

The form of the access and of the exterior space, and therefore the way in which dwellings are linked and stacked, are crucial to the sense of privacy. They have a particular impact on the visual and functional requirements among residents. Noise, however, turns out to play a dominant role in the sense of privacy. Hearing a noise is primordially associated with potential danger or with prey. It puts us on the alert. Remaining in such a state for too long, however, is exhausting.

to a certain extent, clever floor plans can at least reduce noise nuisance.

In residential buildings, bedrooms are not positioned above or next to the neighbours' living room. For the rest, reducing the potential for disruptive contact and air noise primarily relies on construction measures. Within the dwelling itself, regulating the desired relationships between different rooms, places, domains and their privacy gradients traditionally covers a broad range of options. The density of one's housing is not a determining factor per se. Although the size of the dwelling, in combination with the dwelling occupancy, is important for the concept of atmospheres within the dwelling, the privacy of the various residents can also be reasonably protected using sightlines and details such as the turning direction of doors.

individual houses on small parcels, japan

examples of access, munich

view

private roof terrace

views

In their home, people want to relax and be able to shut themselves away from the city. At the same time, they want to maintain their view over their world. From an urban design standpoint, point building seems to offer the most interesting views. The building masses are limited; the porosity of the urban tissue is therefore high. The view, as with coulisses, presents varying depths.

In an urban design fabric of housing blocks, the view is much more monotonous. The wide buildings block the view. For the dwellings themselves, however, the building block conceals a secret, namely the inner garden. In the back reigns peace and quiet – in the front the bustle of the street. In this sense, the view is layered and dually diverse.

Whether the tower block is ultimately as richly varied depends on its slenderness and therefore on the number of dwellings per storey. With two, you have a view on three sides. Windows can be installed in the front, the back and in the side walls. These types of double-oriented buildings are expensive. **developers want three, four or five dwellings per storey. naturally, the number of dwellings increases at the expense of the diversity of the view. you then have to figure out how to provide views on two sides for as many dwellings as possible.**

Or you have to convince the client of the fact that a double double-oriented building is the best choice in terms of cost and quality. The traditional gallery flat is inadequate in terms of views as well. Essentially, the high-rise looks out in one direction only. This applies to an even greater extreme to back-to-back dwellings. In point of fact they are unacceptable. Or you have to compensate in other ways. Liesbeth van der Pol, for instance, has combined the back-to-back with the zigzag dwelling, so that each dwelling has two different views. In addition, these dwellings are distributed over two storeys, so that the view is experienced from different perspectives.

the most ideal view, however, is even more multifaceted and more layered. it looks out not just over the city, but actually over the network, the 'breeding ground'. the dwelling as a 'nest from which to fly'.[10] **a 'barbapapa house', whose limbs extend to get a view of entirely divergent urban spheres: the river, the park, the square, the garden, the sky.**

le corbusier: the framed landscape

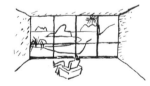

10
smeets, uytenhaak, michel: *la fenêtre* 2007.

collective roof terrace, siemensstadt

EIt is simpler, of course, to distribute habitation over different places. This creates, with the exception of the second home, much more collectivity, as demonstrated by the roof terrace in Una Giornata Particolare or Hans Scharoun's designs in Berlin's Siemensstadt, where the storage facilities, including the deck chairs, are situated along the collective roof terrace.

Architecture can further manipulate and direct this view. Focus it towards what is important. Le Corbusier took this furthest in the Beistégui apartment in Paris. When you look through the periscope, you can see the whole city, but from a single point only. A view that changes as you move through the building is absent. This also applies – in a completely different way– to Ludwig Mies van der Rohe's buildings. The practically empty floor plans and fully glazed façades make the space neutral and preclude a staging – and therefore the surprise – of the view. However beautiful the view may be, it becomes flat.
the dynamics whereby a view is connected to a sense of space are important.

In Gerrit Rietveld's Schröder House in Utrecht, you reach the top of the stairs and are faced with a blank wall – only when you turn can you see out through the large corner window. The effect is magnified by the contrast. We achieved a comparable effect in the flats on Borneo-Sporenburg in Amsterdam's Eastern Harbour District. The front façade is practically closed, except for a relatively small and deep-set window that significantly frames the view. When you reach the top of the stairs, you're looking at that closed wall. Turn your head a quarter turn, however, and you're looking out over the water through a large sliding window and a terrace. The view has been layered. This draws the outside inside more forcefully.

Sometimes we also filter the view. In Haarlem we designed a residential building, the 'veil villa' in Zocher's park. In the Frederikspark, the white villas had to glitter against the green background. If all these dwellings emphatically orient their views towards the park, a public domain will never emerge in that park. The dwellings had to have a somewhat concealed presence. So we fitted them with a veil, made with a silkscreen on glass. The veil is the symbol of the regulation of public and private. Like the veil of the bride and of the widow – though it should be noted that the veil of the bride is the most effective, because white reflects light and dims transparency most.

In making such a façade, you have to figure out how many dots or pixels should be visible (and at what distance) in order to preserve the view from inside outward, yet ensure that no one can see from the outside in.
Finally, varying the shape of the window can also make the view more diverse. In Le Corbusier's designs, the panoramic window and the horizon were often dominant, oriented to the landscape. **using vertical as well horizontal windows, however, combines all sorts of perspectives on the world. a glance into the street, a view of the city under the cloud-strewn sky, and a through-view into the garden.**

rudy uytenhaak: the framed urban landscape

balconies and views of the urban landscape

orientation and natural light

not only can density frustrate privacy, densely built urban tissues can also interfere with natural light penetration.
Dwellings in the Netherlands are now required to meet natural light standards. The angle of obstruction is an important element in this. The greater this angle – in essence, the greater the density – the more limited the amount of natural light coming in. The internal angle of obstruction, however, is also crucial to natural light penetration. Together they form the angle of natural light.

an unfavourable external obstruction can be compensated by a more spacious internal obstruction, that is to say by greater ceiling heights.
An application of this can be found in many historic inner cities. The lower storeys of their dwellings are very open, feature large glass surfaces and high ceilings in order to allow light to penetrate deep into the room. As one goes up, the window openings become smaller and the ceilings lower. The taller the building, after all, the easier it is for light to come in.

building higher ceilings means more expensive façades, so such arrangements are often rejected. however, when light can penetrate deeper into the building, it is possible to make the building deeper and therefore more economical.

different ceiling heights for better penetration of natural light in the lower storeys

adjusting the form of the cross section

Moreover, we gain density in this way, as the laws of density demonstrate. For really deep buildings with shorter façades, there is a tendency to create meandering façades or light yards. This produces greater diversity in incidence of light and provides an opportunity to build more rooms than in a narrow dwelling. The façade-to-floor factor is increased.

Designing the façade and the floor plan behind it is not just a question of natural light but also of orientation. Orientation to the south makes it possible to sit on the balcony and enjoy the sun. Windows to the north, in principle, provide the nicest view, since it is more comfortable to look out with the sun behind you than into it. High-density low-rise dwellings can benefit more from skylights, since in this way natural light penetration does not come at the expense of privacy.
In large collective residential buildings it is often difficult to position the rooms within the internal angles so that sufficient natural light comes in and the orientation is acceptable as well. It's a question of figuring out a puzzle. This is why the design of the Stadionplein project near the former Olympic stadium in Amsterdam was based on corners. To get these right, we set an extra design criterion whereby a corner dwelling can only be unilaterally oriented if it is oriented towards the west. The dwelling will then get the afternoon and evening sun. A dwelling oriented towards the east only gets a little bit of sun in the morning, and that is not consistent with the usual tempo of urban life.

a more rigorous strategy for optimizing incoming natural light is to adapt the shape of the building's cross section.

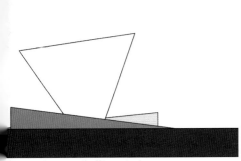

leyweg city council offices, the hague 2004

If there is less natural light, the building has to be less deep. The municipal offices building in The Hague has the shape of a triangle on its point and therefore a small footprint. The ground level remains open. Space is created around the building. Then the building opens upward, like a vase. Towards the light. A little like the way a tree draws its nutrition and water from the ground and light from the sky, the municipal offices building brings in the people who work there from under the building and thus lets in as much natural light as possible from above. After tests in the natural-light rooms, we decided on a special silkscreen on glass for the walls of the atrium. The white pixels on the glass for the top floors are primarily meant to reflect natural light downward, so the pixel pattern up there is dense. The lower you go in the atrium, the more open the print should be, to allow more and more natural light in. By paying a lot of attention to natural light, orientation, privacy and views, it is possible to design buildings that provide adequate compensations for the needed density. Buildings can be open to their surroundings and at the same time provide sufficient space to be able to withdraw from the city.

finding a balance among the four sometimes conflicting parameters can be compared to operating a slide rule. the sliding motion can achieve an ideal or optimum for every location. the priority might be the view for one location and privacy for another. the design derives its specificity and therefore its power from this. achieving this sounds simpler than it is in reality. of course this calls for intuition, for sensitivity. in addition, a great deal of data is imperative.

Such data can be obtained by studying existing buildings, including buildings that predate the twentieth century. Buildings from before the electric light, but also from before building codes and the national building decree. Of course great strides were made during the twentieth-century exodus out of the tenements and slums, making significant gains in terms of light and air. At the same time, some 'cityness' and certainly know-how about light in the city was lost. Know-how that had been applied in historic cities and that is still implicitly present, built and painted. Da Vinci, Canaletto or Delft or Amsterdam houses with their taller ground floors, clever systems of windows and façades based on reflection are examples of this inspirational 'emperical know-how'.

building regulations have made this know-how redundant and in the process made architects lazy.

Ceiling heights and the number of glass openings in the façade, for example, are stipulated in the building decree. They require scarcely any further consideration. Particularly as many clients view these requirements as the feasible maximum and base their budgets on them. The intuition of many architects is therefore focused on meeting the requirements of the building decree and far less on making the dwelling as interesting as possible and thus on deriving optimum benefit out of the environmental factors. As a result, residential buildings have become anaemic.

to make building more richly varied, architects will have to offer more. more quality, that goes without saying, but also more floor space. by designing alternative plans with higher densities than required, architects can create more budget and therefore more freedom for themselves. at the same time, density forces the architect to think more carefully and more deeply about views, natural light, orientation and privacy. designing on automatic pilot, according to the building decree, is not enough. design should again be a matter of study, and figuring out puzzles, and finding the correct balances. the quality of density, or the density of quality.

view and natural light

canaletto

hong kong

9 measures

towards cities full of quality

towards cities full of quality: 9 measures

The snowball effect of 'just a few more houses' is not well understood. And this while the **cumulative effect** of more inhabitants who share their now larger houses with fewer people is visible all around us.

In the last hundred years, the effective per capita surface has grown twelve-fold and is set to grow by a factor of three in the coming decades. The exploding demand for space has heretofore been answered with deconcentration. Liberal policy may have honoured individual claims for space, but it has proved incapable of championing the **collective interest** by creating public spaces of high quality. This way of dealing with space has left the city and the urban sphere both threadbare and diluted, and they have overrun, as it were, the already fragmented countryside.

Instead of sprawling, we should concentrate and cluster. We have to **bring the city back to life**. For the Netherlands, this now seems an almost unnatural move. It is simpler (read: more profitable) to find and build new housing and work areas outside existing city limits. It is the **job of the state** to launch the necessary counter-movement. It will have to stimulate the densification of today's cities.

Densification alone, however, does not automatically produce interesting cities with the required power of attraction. In fact, high densities entail (major) downsides. Architecture has to be able to **eliminate and compensate for the negative spatial effects**. To this end it needs more knowledge about capacity and spatial qualities. This knowledge naturally requires imagination, but also, certainly, observations, typological reconnaissance and fundamental research. The demand for space has to be acknowledged, but also measured and programmed. Imagination, combined with quantitative research in the tradition of Van Lohuizen and Van Eesteren, leads to a foundation for an attractive city.

The following are 9 practical measures that might facilitate and stimulate research into and the design of attractive, spatially interesting, densely built cities.

1

All building developments must provide a justification according to an **NEN standard for density in FSi and GSi values**. This will stimulate consciousness-raising. In addition, these data can be used to develop a **library** containing **a diversity of housing and work environments**, which can be used for disciplined design research and policy.

2

A similar **library** must be set up for the countryside, with a **diversity of rural environments**, providing insight into the value of each for such things as water storage, recreational capacity, agriculture, migratory patterns, a national ecological network and real estate.

3

the links between economics, spatial developments and mobility must be investigated. Are these developments really aimed at integral value augmentation, or are their objectives limited and do they seek only short-term gains? Crunch all the numbers and produce models in order to provide insight into the costs of public space and public transport (land, energy and public services).

4

a stricter policy for the use of space must be developed. At the moment, new residential districts are often based on open-ended scenarios, based on references that are later adjusted to a certain extent. In this, excessively simple guideline numbers are used, such as 100 housing units inside the ring road or 40 housing units per hectare in areas whose boundaries are not always clearly defined. Yet only with **precise considerations of water, greenery and building surface** can the needed diversity in quality and density be created. The **tare telescope** can be a useful instrument in this regard. After all, it visualizes the ratios of net floor space to the land required at various levels of scale. In addition, the tare telescope makes it possible to **compare urban models with different space allocations across these levels of scale**. This can turn it into the basis for interdisciplinary research and effective policy.

5

Within the new, stricter policy, architects must develop scenarios for **attractive living environment**. This entails providing an identity, that is to say **character as well as coherence**, to the work, recreation and housing environments based on landscape structures. Only in this way can an identifiable and legible city be created. A patchwork, lacking an identifiable internal and external quality, can too easily turn into a mess.

6

Administrators must stimulate the development of more, **larger dwellings in the city**. The dwellings being built at the moment are actually too small. Dwellings that are too small, in the cities, lead to social instability. Nieuw West in Amsterdam, but also Sporenburg, are illustrations of this. **financial** incentives, especially, can be provided. This can make the **cost of land inversely proportional to the exploitation** of the land. For instance, when within the same area of land (within the same dynamic envelope) 30 percent more dwellings are built that are 30 per cent larger, the original cost of land is still applied.

7

A city implies that **more dwellings benefit from greater quality**. The valuation of the quality collected in them means that dwellings of equal price are smaller. If more dwellings are built, scarcity will be eased, and larger dwellings will be possible as well. This will **reinforce the appeal of living in the city**. Better and healthier for the people, the city and the country.

8

Larger dwellings can be built more simply by creating **deeper (and higher)** dwellings. These larger building blocks make **greater net densities** attainable.

9

The **expansion capacity** of existing and new housing must be included in the Urban Programme of Requirements.

laws of density

a city is a spatial system that accommodates the mutual proximity of activities, people and their institutions, preferably with flair.

to achieve this, a proper ratio of volume to space is crucial, not just as an absolute 'ideal' percentage, but primarily as a question of distribution, in which particles of mass and space are organized optimally in relation to one another. distributions over different levels of scale overlap and in the process determine the resulting urban tissue.

In this section, 'The Laws of Density', we present a summary of the research into quantitative cohesion. In order to develop intelligent urban tissues in which density and primary spatial quality can be optimized, the laws are intended to define the link among the variables indicated in the definitions. Our initial aim is to look for intensive urban mass density: high FSi values. Ultimately, through an increasingly integral approach in which more qualitative aspects are described by the model, we aim to develop instruments with which typologies of dwellings and other building volumes can be interrogated and ordered in a broader way. The FSi variable is input in order to neutralize the impact of the size of the dwellings and the gross-net ratios of buildings in the first instance.

The premises are fairly primitive to begin with. For natural light, for example, we initially assume an angle of obstruction of 45 degrees. Gradually, the penetration of natural light in buildings becomes a more intelligent component of the conditions under which the patterns emerge.

The densities of four base types of building patterns, regular patterns of
**point building,
strip building,
building blocks
and patio building**
are compared.
In this, the scale of the base type from which the pattern is made up is varied both in depth and in stacking. The FSI values attained with the four patterns are calculated. This provides information on the relationships between building typology, height, depth and density. The values found depend, of course, on the mathematical rules and input values used, but they do provide insight into the nature of these patterns. First, the primary building patterns are described quantitatively in spreadsheets, step by step, by varying their stacking or building depth or angle of obstruction.

patterns and profiles
Patterns describe the distribution of the buildings over the base. Profiles describe the building height occupied by these patterns in the third dimension. In other words they describe the cross section of the buildings. In this, the building height is still considered the result of simple, geometrical stacking. In addition, for this stacking the angle of obstruction, building depth and ceiling height are kept constant. For the patterns, too, only the building depth is varied initially.

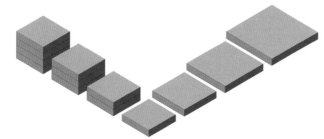

densification by stacking   densification by expanding

profiles and natural light

Of course, the quality of natural light of a shallow, low-ceilinged storey is not the same as that of a deep, high-ceilinged storey, as assumed in the primary models. And what if the ceiling height and dwelling width are varied, with a deeper or shallower penetration of natural light as a result?

profiles and the interior-exterior ratios in relation to ceiling height

In studying density based on profiles, we usually come up against the angle of obstruction as determinative for the ratio of space to volumes. It defines the profile of the exterior space left open in relation to the height of the buildings facing it. But the depth of the buildings also has an impact, for example, on the penetration of natural light at this building depth. Natural light also depends on the ceiling height, and therefore the impact of the ceiling height on the building depth and with it the density is also examined. The proportion of the profile of the interior space in relation to the exterior space remains essential. Low and/or deep interior spaces are relatively more obstructed than high, shallow spaces.

This obstruction primarily concerns the light penetration, but also the privacy, as well as the possibilities for this in retaining light yield.

natural light or sunlight?

In determining the quality of natural light in a building or district we make a distinction between directly entering sunlight and the degree to which diffuse natural light penetrates a space. In a diffuse sky, sunlight is evenly distributed in all directions as a result of refraction of the sun's rays by clouds, and orientation does not yet play a role. Incidentally, the quantity of light at the horizon, because of the angle of refraction with the atmosphere, is three times less than that from directly above. About 70 per cent of the time, the Netherlands experiences a diffuse sky. The fact that diffuse natural light is independent of orientation and that for the greater part of the year only this primary diffuse natural light is present is the most significant reason to relate the quality of natural light of building, first and foremost, to situations featuring diffuse natural light.

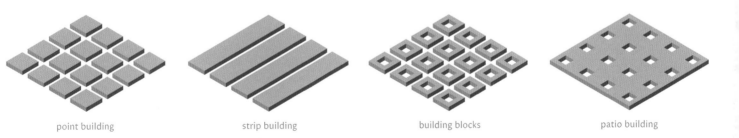

point building strip building building blocks patio building

the densities of four basic types of building patterns are compared

GSi

The Ground Space Index (GSi) indicates the relationship between the footprint of the building and the available site area. The building percentage is a result of the building pattern and the dimensions of these patterns. Point, strip, block and patio building patterns are the typical base forms of building patterns.

FSi

The Floor Space Index (FSi) is a ratio that indicates what the realized quantity of floor space (GFA) is in relation to the ground space/site. Mathematically it is equal to the building percentage × the stacking factor.

profile density

Just as the GSi is based on the footprint, the profile density is the surface area, as it were, of the cross section of an imaginarily extruded building. The FSi per horizontal metre of the cross section can be determined; we call this the profile density: FSi/m^1 of profile.
The profile density is the quotient of the surface area developed per horizontal metre of the cross-section, and this surface area increases along with the open space.
FSi/m^1 = number of storeys (n)*building depth (d)/(building depth + street width (s))

façade index

The façade index stands for the ratio of the façade surface area to the gross floor area (GFA): the number of square metres of façade per square metre of floor. Façade Index (Gi) = façade surface area/gross floor area (GFA)

angle of obstruction

The angle of obstruction is determinative for the ratio of space to mass in a profile In this we distinguish between the external angle of obstruction (b), which defines the 'lower shadow', and the internal angle of obstruction (i), which is defined by the ceiling height inside the dwelling: the 'upper shadow'.
The angle of obstruction is used to determine what the profile of the exterior space left open is in zoning plans and building codes, and therefore the proportion of open space and the height of facing buildings.

angle of natural light

The angle of natural light (l) is the angle between the external and internal angle of obstruction (l = b − i). The result of these two values is the projection of the light that penetrates directly, when you ignore reflection inside the volume.

links

Density, that is to say a high FSi value, is created by stacking storeys based on a high building percentage (for example, surface-filling or fringe buildings).

The FSi is primarily determined by the building percentage, stacking factor and angle of obstruction.

The building percentage is determined by the building depth and the pattern of built/unbuilt space.

The angle of obstruction is determined by the pattern of built/unbuilt space, as well as the profile of the ceiling height and the stacking factor.

The façade index is determined by the pattern of built and unbuilt space and the ceiling height.

The potency of the interior-exterior relationships of light and view are determined by the façade index. Externally (outside), the angle of obstruction determines the upper limit of this potency.

The angle of natural light determines the depth of penetration of light into the interior.

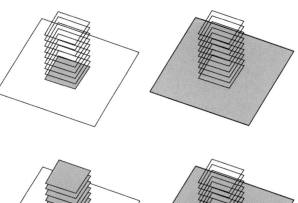

GSi = footprint in m² /site in m² (illustration: permeta, amsterdam)

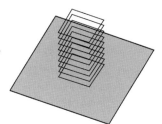

FSi = GFA/site in m² (illustration: permeta, amsterdam)

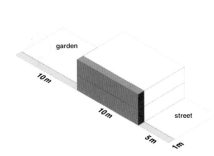

profile density: a building 10 m and two storeys high, on a street of 10 m (2×5 m) and a garden of 10 m, realizes, on average, a floor space of 20 m² in 25 m² of space. the FSi / m¹ is therefore 0.8

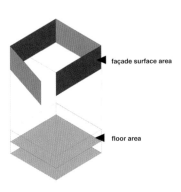

Façade Index (Fi) =
façade surface area/Gross Floor Area (GFA)

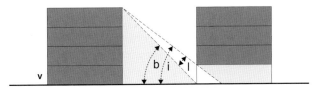

angle of obstruction and angle of natural light
v = a given ceiling height
b = external angle of obstruction
i = internal angle of obstruction
angle of natural light l = b − i

law 1
the density (FSi) increases by stacking higher and making buildings deeper.

In all four building patterns, the combination of stacking higher and building deeper results in a higher density than when only one of these strategies is applied.

The graphs show all the combinations of the number of storeys (1 to 50) and depths (1 to 50) for each of the four patterns. The graph on the right shows what happens to the density as depth increases and the number of storeys increases.

If the depth is shallow, or the amount of storeys low, the density hardly reacts to changes in the other variable. Only the combination of both shows a longer effective growth of the FSi.

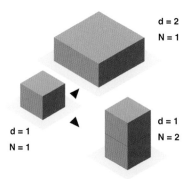

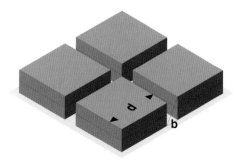

explanation: the mathematical model assumes two variables:
N = number of storeys
d = fringe depth

the above example shows how the basis of the point pattern (an object 1 storey high and 1 m deep) is expanded to an object either 2 storeys high or 2 m deep.

in addition, several constant input values were used:
b = angle of obstruction of 45° to start with
v = ceiling height of 3 m
n = ratio of length to width of 1 to start with

the distance between the objects is determined by the height of the object and the external angle of obstruction b

the height is determined by the number of storeys and their ceiling height

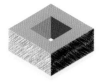

point

strip and building block

patio

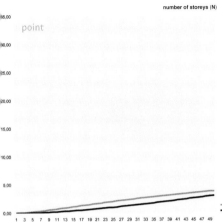

point

number of storeys (N)

depth (d)

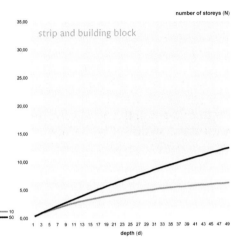

strip and building block

number of storeys (N)

depth (d)

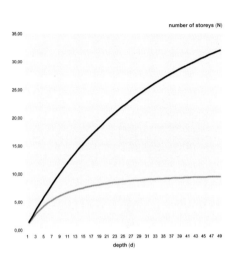

number of storeys (N)

depth (d)

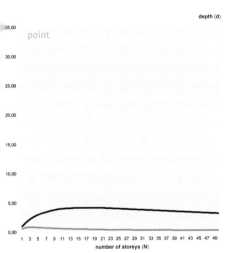

point

depth (d)

number of storeys (N)

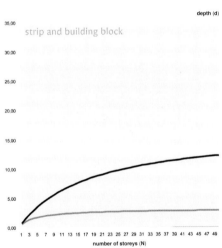

strip and building block

depth (d)

number of storeys (N)

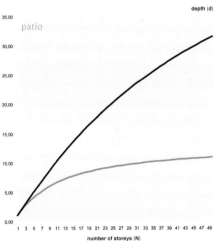

patio

depth (d)

number of storeys (N)

comparison of density based on
comparable building depth (d)
plotted against a number of storeys (N)

the graphs show that with a
comparable building depth d,
the point building pattern attains the lowest FSi,
the strip and the building block equal each other in FSi,
and the patio attains the highest FSi

past a certain point, the bottom lines in the graphs
(d = very low) (N = very small) run virtually horizontal.
this is most apparent in the patio, to a lesser degree
in the strip and the building block and least of all in
the point pattern

law 2
with a constant angle of obstruction, the increase in density (FSi) slows down as stacking or building depth increases.

In the strip, the building block and the patio, building higher and\or deeper always produces a higher FSi. As the depth and the number of storeys increase, however, the increase in the FSi slows down. From this point on, building higher or deeper has little effect.

In point building, building deeper always produces a higher density, but with a noticeable trend. Lower blocks produce a higher density with lesser depth than higher blocks. Only as the blocks get deeper, therefore, it is worthwhile to build higher.

point

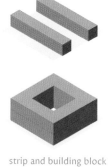

strip and building block

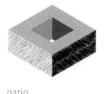

patio

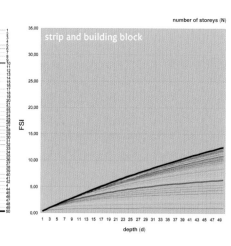

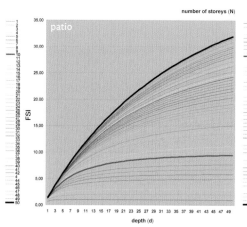

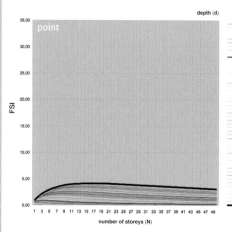

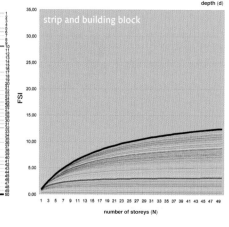

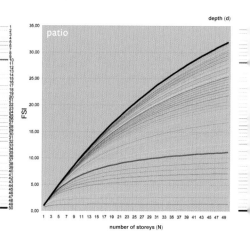

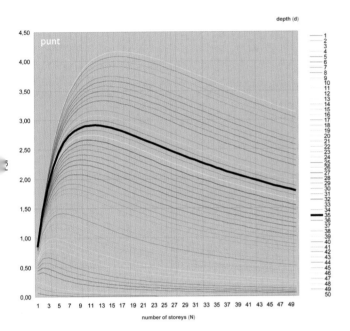

depth (d)

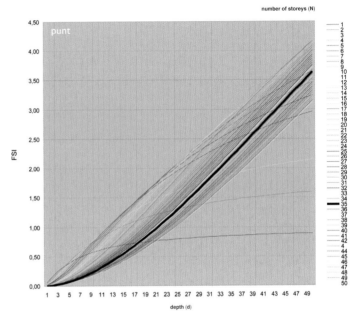

number of storeys (N)

the point is the only pattern that features a maximum. for every depth there is a given number of storeys that produces a maximum FSi. the FSi reaches its maximum value when the space between the objects is equal to the depth of the object (see figure below right). for instance, a point object 50 m deep achieves its highest density at 17 storeys (17 * 3 m = 51 m).

a notable effect is that the increase in FSi only begins after a short run-up for the small blocks, and that this run-up requires increasingly large blocks as the number of storeys increases.

the result is the creation of intersections where equal FSi values can be achieved. for instance, in a point pattern 21 m deep, objects 1 storey high attain the same density as objects 50 storeys high. so we can conclude that with these measures of density there are multiple models of point building that feature the same capacity, yet which we would value entirely in entirely different ways

this graph shows how the density of a point pattern of 35 storeys (black line) develops as the building depth is increased. the upper lines on the graphs are close together; this means that as the depth and the number of storeys increase, the FSi increases more and more slowly. at a constant fringe depth, the FSi increases more and more slowly as the stacking increases.

at an equal number of storeys, the FSi also increases more and more slowly as the fringe depth increases

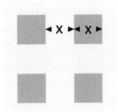

point building has a maximum.
the maximum density is reached in the point pattern when the distance between the objects (at 45 degrees, equal to the building height) is equal to depth of the block (see also the graph at upper right)

law 3
with a constant façade index, the three basic patterns of patios, strips and building blocks produce an equal density. tower blocks feature the lowest density.

In order to compare the four building typologies, the FSis of the four patterns must first be laid out next to one another, based on a comparable building depth (Law 1 figure).
This shows that patio building (with a constant angle of obstruction and stacking factor) can attain the highest density, while point building produces the lowest density. The strip and the building block fall between the two. This is true of both FSi and GSi.

However, the internal corners in patio building result in an unequally dispersed quality of light. In the pattern for the patio, a relatively large quantity of mass is placed contiguously. The result is the creation of many dark spaces in this pattern. The high density of the patio is attained at the expense of the quantity of natural light than can penetrate the block. The next step, therefore, is to determine which building type produces the highest density when the same potential 'quality of natural light' operates in all.

Rather than compare the building depth of the four patterns, their Façade Index was compared. The Façade Index (Gi) is the ratio between the surface of the façade and the gross floor area (GFA). This ratio has an impact on the potential to draw in natural light through the façade and therefore serves as a baseline reference for the primary 'natural light quality' level. This makes the Façade Index a crucial factor in the potential density of equivalent urban tissues.

If the depth is corrected according to a consistent Façade Index (and constant stacking and angle of obstruction), the strip building pattern, building block pattern and patio pattern produce equal FSi values. Only the point building pattern stands out with a lower density. The potentials of the point pattern were therefore examined in greater detail in Law 4.

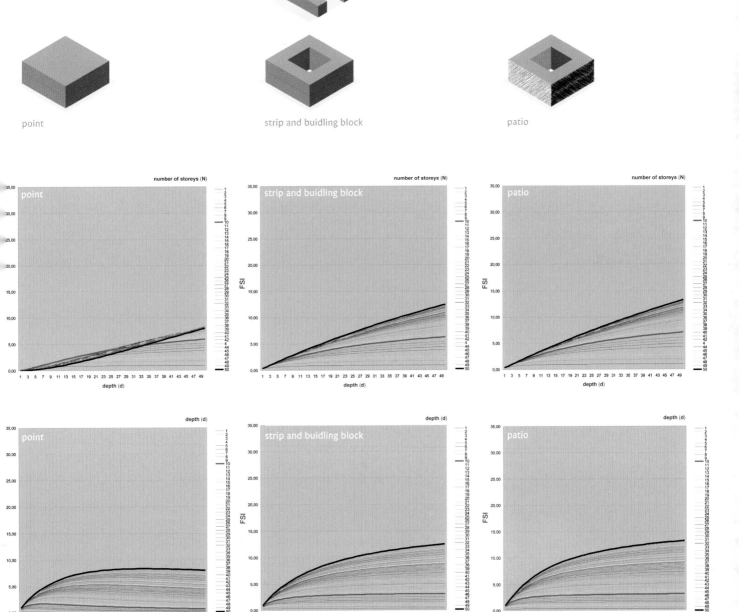

point

strip and buidling block

patio

comparison of density based on comparable façade index. fringe depth (d) plotted against a number of storeys (N)

when the depth of 4 patterns is modified so that the ratio of the façade surface area to the GFA remains equal (this results in an equal Fi), we can see that differences in maximum attainable FSi become much smaller than when the depth of the building block fringe is kept constant. compare the above series with those of law 2

law 4
point building, optimized as a checkerboard, produces the highest FSi.

In point building, as in the other three patterns, making buildings deeper always produces a higher density. Making buildings higher, however, does not always result in a higher density with point building. For every depth, there is a certain number of storeys that produces a maximum FSi. The FSi reaches its maximum value at an angle of obstruction of 45°, when the depth of the object is equal to its height.

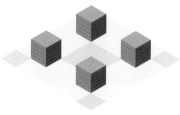

'empty space'

This maximum is caused by 'empty spaces' in the point building pattern. These 'empty spaces' at the inter-sections of the imaginary streets in the pattern grow as the towers get higher, and, with a constant angle of obstruction, distances between the towers must be increased.

In order to optimize the point building pattern, we looked at how these 'empty spaces' might be filled by increasing the density of the pattern at the intersections. This was done in two different ways, the so-called checkerboard and chessboard patterns. Both showed that an FSi equivalent to that of strip building can be achieved by increasing density at the 'intersections'.

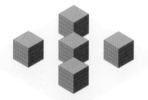

We then looked again at how the FSi that can be attained with the checkerboard pattern behaves in a comparison based on equal façade indices and therefore equivalent primary natural light quality. Results show that the checkerboard, in certain combinations in ratio, can now produce even higher FSis than the other three building types.

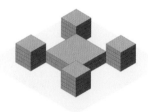

for point building, the impact of filling in empty space on FSi is explained (see next page). this filling in is done in two different ways; we call the first the checkerboard pattern (maximum filling in of the empty space with point building of the same dimensions as the base pattern) and the second is the chessboard pattern (maximum filling in of the empty space with point building of variable dimensions)

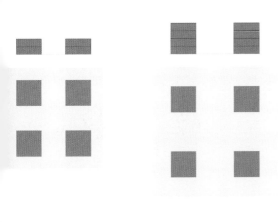
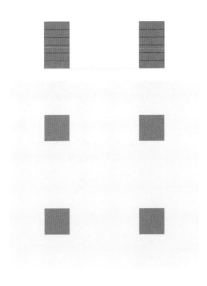

point building base pattern. the empty spaces are filled in in different ways in the following pattern

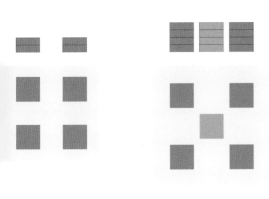
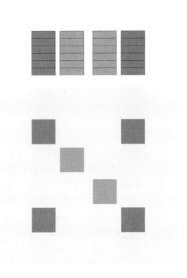

the checkerboard pattern fills the empty spaces with the same building bricks as those of the base pattern

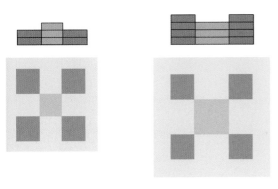
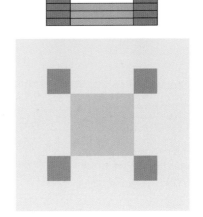

the chessboard pattern fills the empty spaces by filling in the spaces between the buildings completely. the form and height of these new buildings is then determined by the distance between the buildings, which is equal to the depth of the point from the base pattern. this produces different pieces or building bricks. both modifications are therefore a superimposition of point buildings

point

checkerboard

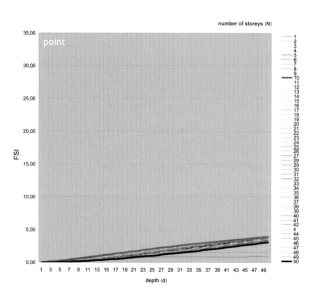

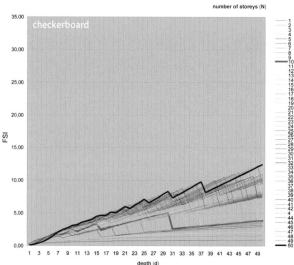

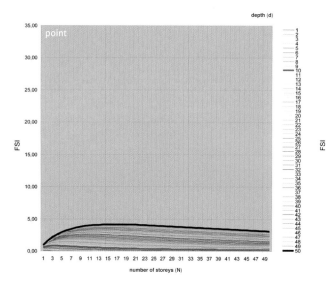

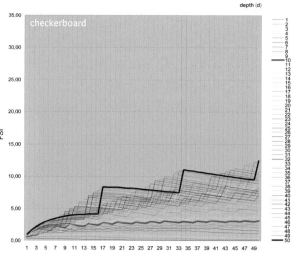

comparison of the densities of different point patterns. equal building depth (d) plotted against a number of storeys (N)

when the empty space in the point pattern is filled in according to the checkerboard pattern or the chessboard pattern, this produces an FSi that matches that of the strip. in the graph of the checkerboard, the graph spikes upward at the moments at which space is produced to add a new point to the pattern. at these moments the pattern is filled to maximum, and the density matches that of the strip. the difference, however, is that more façade surface area is realized per GFA in the checkerboard pattern

chessboard

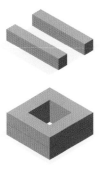

strip and building block

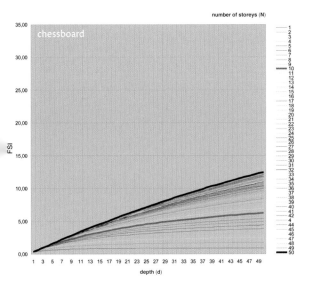

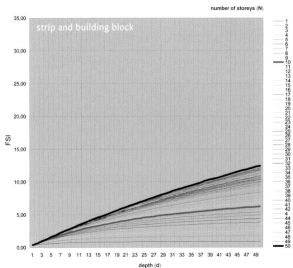

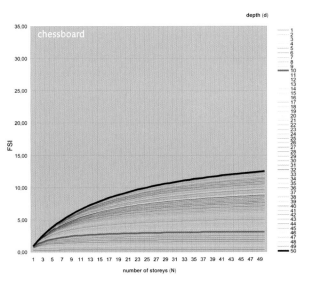

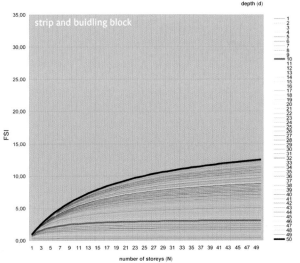

the graph of the chessboard follows that of the strip.
in this pattern, therefore, the same FSi is realized as
in the strip building. the chessboard pattern does
have a greater façade index than the strip and\or the
building block

point

checkerboard

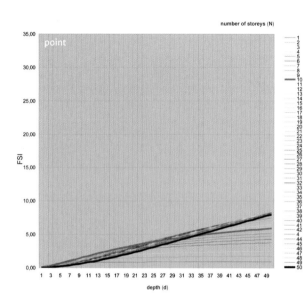

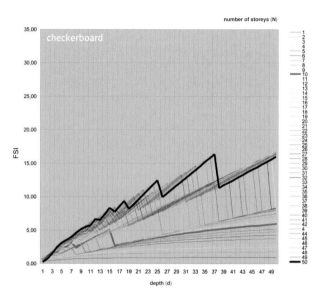

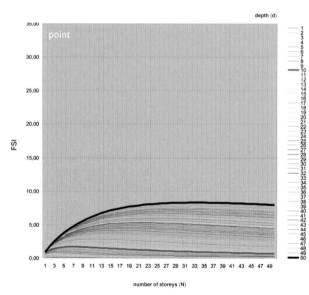

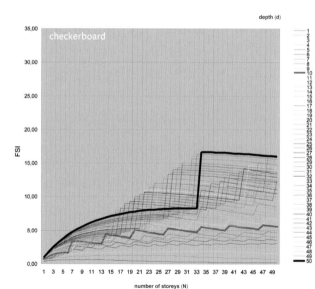

strip and building block

patio

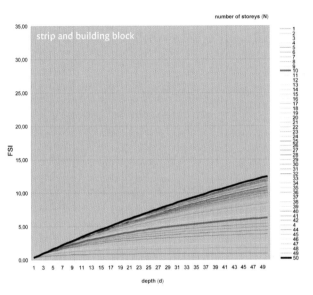

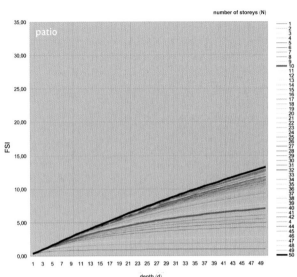

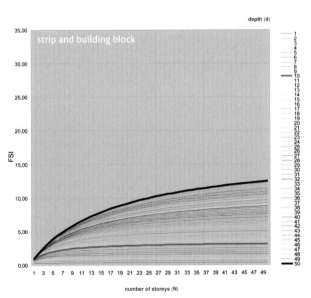

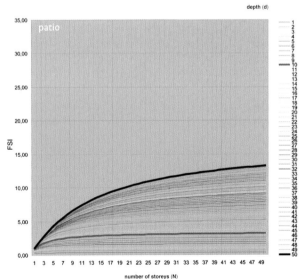

comparison of point patterns based on a comparable
façade index. building depth (d) plotted against a
number of storeys (N).
the checkerboard compared with the base patterns
based on a comparable façade index.
if the building depth for the checkerboard is adjusted
so that a façade index equal to that of the strip or the
building block, the checkerboard pattern can, in certain
combinations of depth and number of storeys, produce
a higher density with the same quality of natural light
than with the point, strip, building block and patio

law 5
FSi is independent of scale.
low and shallow storeys produce the same FSi as high and deep storeys, if the façade index is kept constant.
if, however, the building height is limited, low storeys of shallow depth produce a higher FSi.

What are the consequences for density when the ratio of building depth to ceiling height is kept constant? Previous research into the relationship between building type and density has shown that making buildings deeper, regardless of the building type, always produces a higher density. Building deeper, however, also produces a lower Façade Index. There is, after all, less façade surface per square metre of GFA, with a lower level of natural light quality as a result.

The mathematical model was therefore adjusted so as to link the ceiling height to the depth of the building in a set ratio. This simple condition ensures that the natural light quality is kept more constant (by keeping the spatial ratio between v and d constant in the interior).

If we opt for a higher ceiling height, for instance 4 m instead of 3 m, the scale of the cross sections changes, but not the profile density (FSi/m¹).

The conclusion is that when the ceiling height and the building depth are increased proportionally, the Façade Index remains constant and this has no impact on the FSi. The FSi is independent of scale, as it were. We then posed the question of whether at a set, maximum building height H, it is more efficient, in terms of density, to build deeper and higher or instead shallower and lower storeys. To determine this, the building height H was added to the mathematical model for the strip building pattern. This showed that shallower and lower storeys produced a slightly higher FSi. In shallow models, after all, the total template is smaller than in deep variants. They can therefore be placed in a denser pattern, and this produces a higher FSi.

with a constant ratio of d and v, every d results in the same FSi. the FSi is scale-independent

with a constant ratio of d and v and a fixed total building height H the shallow, low variant produces a higher FSi compared to the deep high variant

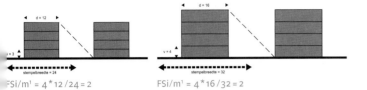

$$FSi/m^1 = 4*12/24 = 2$$

$$FSi/m^1 = 4*16/32 = 2$$

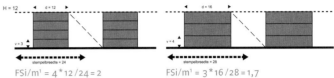

$$FSi/m^1 = 4*12/24 = 2$$

$$FSi/m^1 = 3*16/28 = 1,7$$

an increase in the ceiling height has no impact on the profile density (FSi/m) when the ratio of the ceiling height to the building depth is fixed. when the total height H (v*N) is kept constant, the same quantity of GFA is realized at every depth in strip building.
this is because of the constant ratio of the ceiling height to the depth, which means that at a given height a high ceiling height results in a small number of storeys and a great depth. a low ceiling height results in a large number of storeys and a small depth. because of the fixed ratio, therefore, every variant has the same quantity of GFA

because of the constant height, every variant has the same distance. in shallow variants, the total template is therefore smaller than in deeper variants, so that these can be positioned closer together in a pattern, which produces a higher FSi. this can be seen in the figure below, in which the H and FSi for strip building are given. heights of 10 m, 50 m and 100 m are shown

depth comparison for strip building

d = depth of the strip

The table below gives the FSi for strip building. Rows are N = number of storeys (1–50); columns are d = depth of the strip (1–50). Within each row the FSi value is essentially constant across all depths:

N = number of storeys	FSi (constant across d = 1…50)
1	0.83
2	1.43
3	1.88
4	2.22
5	2.50
6	2.73
7	2.92
8	3.08
9	3.21
10	3.33
11	3.44
12	3.53
13	3.61
14	3.68
15	3.75
16	3.81
17	3.86
18	3.91
19	3.96
20	4.00
21	4.04
22	4.07
23	4.11
24	4.14
25	4.17
26	4.19
27	4.22
28	4.24
29	4.26
30	4.29
31	4.31
32	4.32
33	4.34
34	4.36
35	4.38
36	4.39
37	4.40
38	4.42
39	4.43
40	4.44
41	4.46
42	4.47
43	4.48
44	4.49
45	4.50
46	4.51
47	4.52
48	4.53
49	4.54
50	4.55

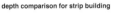

H = 10   H = 50   H = 100

FSi for strip building at different total building heights (H). heights of 10 m, 50 m and 100 m are shown. when in the model the ceiling height v is made dependent on the depth d, the FSi increases as a result of the increase in the number of storeys and the GSi decreases; this increase is the same for both indices for every depth

law 6
the combination of making a building deep and a high angle of obstruction (above 30°) reduces the need to place buildings closer to one another, for the FSi does not increase linearly in this instance.

So far, we've looked at how the FSi of the different building types is influenced by the depth and height of building. The building height was the result of the amount of storeys, with a set ceiling height of 3 m. The distance between buildings was determined by the angle of obstruction, which was set at 45°, because this is the angle generally assumed to allow enough natural light into the building at ground level. The question now, however, is to what degree the angle of obstruction influences the FSi.

Greater external angles of obstruction increase the FSi but decrease the potential output of natural light inside. In deeper buildings with an equal angle of obstruction, the FSi also increases and the actual distribution of natural light per GFA also decreases.

In all four patterns, it is clear that when buildings are made deeper, increasing the angle of obstruction has less effect on the FSi. If you make buildings deep, therefore, it is of relatively little benefit to the FSi to place buildings very close to one another. If the angle of obstruction is low and there are fewer storeys, growth is more or less constant. Raising the angle of obstruction (placing buildings closer together) has a greater effect on the FSi if there are more storeys, especially if the angle of obstruction is 60° or higher (a building density which is hardly ever reached).

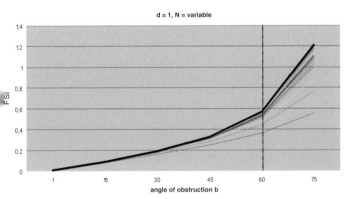

d = 1, N = variable

x-axis: angle of obstruction b
y-axis: FSi

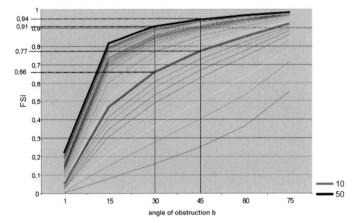

N = 1, d = variable

x-axis: angle of obstruction b
y-axis: FSi

Legend:
— 10
— 50

with a greater number of storeys N, the increase in the angle of obstruction (erecting buildings closer together) has a greater effect on the FSi than with a smaller number of storeys N.
However, this sharper rise in the FSi only occurs in the last part of the graph (from about 60 degrees), and is therefore not very relevant to real situations

with a large d (making buildings deeper) the FSi rises in particular in the first part of the graph and less in the second part. this means that when buildings are made deeper a greater angle of obstruction (erecting buildings closer together) has relatively little impact on the FSi past a certain point. thus if you make buildings deep, relatively little gain is achieved in the FSi even if you erect buildings very close together.
in strip building, we can see that, for example, an increase in the angle of natural light from 30° to 45° at d = 50 (black line) results in an increase in the FSi of 0.03 (from 0.91 to 0.94) and at d = 10 (white line) in an increase of 0.11 (from 0.66 to 0.77)

law 7

with a constant exterior angle of obstruction, the depth of penetration of natural light increases as the street width decreases. formula:
the theoretical depth of penetration of natural light = street width * ceiling height / (facing building height – height of own ceiling in relation to ground surface level)

The combined effect of obstruction and ceiling height is studied by varying the building height, depth and angle of obstruction.
This way, we can study the impact of the number of storeys on the density with a set angle of obstruction (or the ratio of street width to building height). The ratio of building depth to ceiling height was also kept constant. It plays a role in determining the degree of natural light penetration.

Say the angle of obstruction is 45°, as in earlier analyses. This produces the following formula, derived from the formula for profile density:
$FSi/m^1 = d.N / (d + N.v)$
In which:
N = number of storeys
v = ceiling height
d = building depth

The relation between the angle of obstruction and the penetration of diffuse natural light is explained in the illustration on the following page. The maximum penetration of natural light is defined by:
- the street width from façade to façade;
- the height of the opposite building;
- the ceiling height of the specific storey;
- the location of the floor of the specific storey in relation to the ground surface level.

Up to now, we assumed that a constant angle of obstruction allows us to compare density results, but now we will differentiate between external and internal angles of obstruction.

The external angle of obstruction is determined by the street width and the height of the building across the street. The internal angle of obstruction depends on the ceiling height and the external angle of obstruction, as well as on which storey of the building you are on.

From this, the following mathematical relationship can be established:
Theoretical depth of penetration = street width * ceiling height / (opposite building height – height of ceiling in relation to ground surface level)
Or, put another way:
Theoretical depth of penetration = street width * ceiling height / (street width * tang external angle of obstruction – height of ceiling in relation to ground surface level)
The formula demonstrates that the same external angle of obstruction and ceiling height can produce a different output of natural light, as a result of a different street width and building height. Take a street width of 10 m and an external angle of obstruction of 45°. At a ceiling height of 3 m, the theoretical depth of penetration on the ground floor is 4.3 m. At a street width of 20 m, an external angle of obstruction of 45° and a ceiling height of 3 m, the penetration depth is 3.5 m.

natural light simulation
Natural light simulations clearly show that the higher the storey, the higher the incidence of natural light. The results of the natural light simulations also show that the 1 Lux ISO line closely approximates the theoretical penetration depth if the reflections of walls, floors and ceilings are excluded (in other words, if they are black).
Simulations also show that, at the same external angle of obstruction and ceiling height, there can be different natural light outputs as a result of a different street width. An effect we expected based on mathematical relationships. The simulation results are explained on the following page.

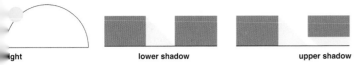

light   lower shadow   upper shadow

lower shadow and upper shadow

external angle of obstruction 45°, 1 storey: 100% light penetration

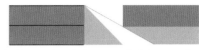

external angle of obstruction 45°, 2 storeys: 41% light penetration

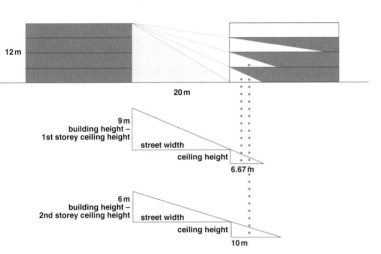

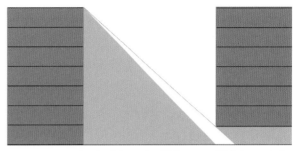

external angle of obstruction 45°, 7 storeys: 26% light penetration

the external angle of obstruction (in this case 30°) and the ceiling height (or façade height, in this case 3 m) determine what is called the internal angle of obstruction on the various storeys (for example, 24° on the ground floor in this case) and with it the extent to which natural light penetrates into the storey. In this case this is 6.6 m on the ground floor and 10 m on the first floor

simulation results show that the natural light yield at the same external angle of obstruction can vary according to the street width. profiles with narrow streets show an advantage in relation to wide streets (assuming that the ceiling height is the same). simulations were carried out without interior reflections.

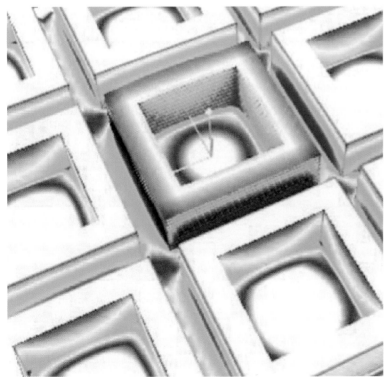

the results of these natural light simulations show that the 1-lux isoline approaches the theoretical depth of penetration quite well at the various external angles of obstruction. in this case the calculations were made for a building block of 10 storeys with a street width of about 30 m. the simulations did not take into account reflections from the interior or exterior (the reflection coefficients of the walls, floors and ceilings are 0%). these results were then compares with patio and point building patterns with the same GSi and building height (and therefore the same FSi) in order to study what ratio of mass to space (streets and\or courtyards) produces the best natural light results – in general, but in particular in the lower storeys. as a building pattern shows a greater number of smaller perforations, the building depth (at a constant GSi) will decrease and the façade index will increase, which in principle is conducive to natural light penetration. however, as the streets and the light yards get smaller, the external angle of obstruction does increase at an equal number of storeys. this decreases the light intensity on the façade. the idea, therefore, is to find an optimum between the building depth and the scale of the spaces between the buildings.

source: 'gevel en stad' study, delft university of technology, faculty of architecture, in cooperation with building physics and urbanism

law 8
the lit surface area of a building strip with unobstructed, unilaterally lit spaces is in linear proportion to the façade index.

What influence does the Façade Index (and the height and depth of the storey) have on the penetration of natural light into a building? With the help of a formula, the theoretical natural light penetration depth can be measured per storey – and thus the percentage of the floor area that is lit and that which stays dark.

Take, for instance, a strip building with a building depth of 10 m, in which the dwellings are arranged back-to-back. If the external angle of obstruction is 30° and the ceiling height is 2.8 m, the total building height depends on the width of the street; 2.8 m (1 storey) if the street is 5 m wide, 5.8 m if the street is 10 m wide and 17.3 m if the street is 30 m wide. The Façade Index can be derived from the height of the façade and the depth of the building. In this example the Façade Index is 0.288. A 30-m-wide street and 17.3-m-high building (with an external angle of obstruction of 30°) results in five storeys and a building depth of 10 m. The theoretical natural light penetration depth per storey is: 6 m on the ground floor, 7.5 m on the first floor and 10 m on the second, third, fourth and fifth floors (at a ceiling height of $17.3/6 = 2.88$ m). The maximum penetration depth can never exceed the building depth, 10 m in this case.

In the situation sketched above, 10.8 per cent of the GFA receives no natural light (6.6/60). The FSi per metre, the profile density, is 2.4 (GFA/(0.5 * width of the street + building depth), in which the GFA is equal to the number of storeys multiplied by the building depth). Rather than using the GFA, we can also use the lit GFA (53.5 m² rather than 60 m²). In that case, the lit FSi per metre is 2.1.

The Lit Façade Index could be defined in the same way: surface area of the façade/lit GFA. In that case the Façade Index is 0.32. This is obviously less economical that the 0.28.

This analysis can be repeated for various angles of obstruction and street widths.

The decrease in the depth of penetration is the greatest at high angles of obstruction. The difference between the floor area and the lit floor area increases along with the increase in the angle of obstruction. In other words, the higher the angle of obstruction, the more dark floor area. The FSi/m[1]-lit tends to a value between 2.5 and 3.5, depending on the angle of obstruction of the examined strip building with a building depth of 10 m.

The graph on the next page shows how the Lit Façade Index increases along with the external angle of obstruction (assuming that the GFA is equal to the lit floor area). Take, for instance, a lit surface area of 50 m². If the external angle of obstruction is 30°, the surface area of the façade has to be circa 25 m², if it is 45° the surface area of the façade has to be circa 40 m², and 60° leads to circa 60 m². The Façade Indexes are respectively 0.5, circa 0.75 and 1.25. (see the graph on page 115)

luminous intensity
We've concentrated on the position of the 50-Lux ISO line because it is the most representative for the degree of natural light that penetrates spaces. The luminous intensity is also an important factor in how space is experienced. The narrower the street, the lower the initial value of the luminous intensity at the façade.

Measuring the average luminous intensity is a numeric indication of the quality of natural light in a space. Natural light simulations in 50 m² spaces with varying façade widths prove, for instance, that the average luminous intensity in a space increases linearly along with the Façade Index.

penetration of natural light depending on the width and height of the space
(without external obstruction)

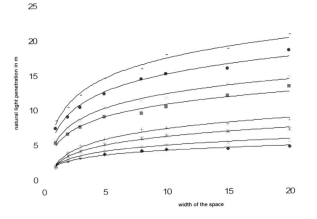

- 50 lux at a ceiling height of 5 m
- 50 lux at a ceiling height of 4 m
- 50 lux at a ceiling height of 3 m
- 50 lux at a ceiling height of 2.5 m
- 500 lux at a ceiling height of 2.5 m
- 500 lux at a ceiling height of 3 m
- 500 lux at a ceiling height of 4 m
- 500 lux at a ceiling height of 5 m

penetration of natural light (in horizontal metres)
depending on the façade width of the space if there is
no obstruction. the position of 50 as well as 500 lux
is given for different ceiling heights.
the simulations were carried out without taking interior
reflections into account and without obstruction of
natural light penetration by the facade.
the same simulations were carried out with external
angles of obstruction of 30°, 45° and 60°

penetration of natural light depending on the width and height of the space
(without external obstruction)

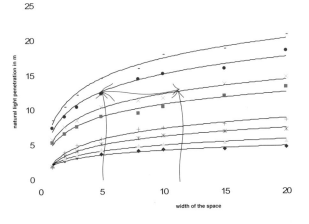

- 50 lux at a ceiling height of 5 m
- 50 lux at a ceiling height of 4 m
- 50 lux at a ceiling height of 3 m
- 50 lux at a ceiling height of 2.5 m
- 500 lux at a ceiling height of 2.5 m
- 500 lux at a ceiling height of 3 m
- 500 lux at a ceiling height of 4 m
- 500 lux at a ceiling height of 5 m

comparable depth of penetration of natural light
in a space 5 m wide and 4 m high, versus a space 11 m
wide and 3 m high
(without external obstruction and reflection)

law 9

with a limited angle of obstruction, low spaces produce relatively better lit surface area than high spaces with an equal façade index. however, when the angle of obstruction is greater than 30°, there is little or no significant difference in the percentage of lit surface area in spaces with a high but narrow façade and spaces with a low but wide façade.

What we now want to know is what effect making spaces higher and deeper or lower and shallower has on the lit floor area.

influence of spatial ratios

In addition to the external angle of obstruction and façade height (and the resulting internal angle of obstruction), the façade width also determines how deep natural light can penetrate into a space. The lateral walls of a space function as 'blinkers' (vertically). The mathematical approximations cited in the preceding laws therefore apply only in very wide storeys. In such instances, there is no obstruction of natural light penetration by the (lateral) walls of the spaces. For this ninth law, we are investigating to what degree the width of the space obstructs the penetration of natural light.

For this analysis, spaces of different widths (1, 2, 3, 5, 8, 10, 15 and 20 m) are considered. Using natural light simulations, we examine how deep natural light penetrates into the space at different ceiling heights. These simulations were performed without obstruction and with external angles of obstruction of 30°, 45° and 60°.

The simulations demonstrate that the penetration of natural light increases logarithmically in proportion to the width of the space. In other words, this is a case of diminishing returns.

This link can be seen in both the position of the 500-Lux ISO line and that of the 50-Lux ISO line – whereby the 50-Lux ISO line is naturally set deeper into the space than the 500-Lux ISO line. It turns out that it is more effective to make spaces wider than to make them higher. Compare, for instance, an 5-m-wide and 4-m-high space to one that is 3 m high. For natural light to penetrate to the same depth, the 3-m-high space has to be 11 m wide (see graph on page 113). This shows that, as far as the façade surface is concerned, it is more effective to build a low and wide space than a high and narrow one. The Façade Index of both situations is respectively 0.32 and 0.24 (20/5 × 12.5 versus 33/11 × 12.5). The wider space needs relatively less façade surface to achieve the same incidence of natural light for the same GFA (if there is no external obstruction).

The logarithmic link (diminishing returns) between the penetration depth of natural light and the width of the space remains with external angles of obstruction. However, the impact of the width of the space is clearly less with a greater external angle of obstruction.

As the space gets wider, the measured value approaches the theoretical penetration depth. In a space 1 m wide, natural light penetrates 20 to 30 per cent less far into the space than theoretically expected. In a space 10 m wide, this falls to only 5 to 10 per cent.

We can use the above results from the natural light simulations to study the relationship between lit floor space and the façade surface in more detail. The result is shown in the graph on the next page.
It is clear that there is no difference (or only a negligible difference) between deep spaces with a high but narrow façade and a shallower space with a low but wide façade when the external angle of obstruction is greater than 30°. This is in contrast with situations without external angles of obstruction, in which wider spaces prove more effective than high spaces.

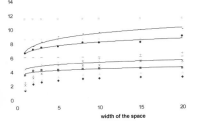

penetration of natural light, depending on the width and height of the space (30° obstruction)

- ● 500 lux at a ceiling height of 2.5 m
- ■ 50 lux at a ceiling height of 2.5 m
- ⋯ 500 lux at a ceiling height of 3 m
- ⋯ 50 lux at a ceiling height of 3 m
- × 500 lux at a ceiling height of 4 m
- ● 50 lux at a ceiling height of 4 m
- ＋ 500 lux at a ceiling height of 5 m
- ⋅ 50 lux at a ceiling height of 5 m
- — max, 3 m
- — max, 4 m
- — max, 5 m

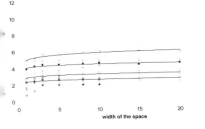

penetration of natural light, depending on the width and height of the space (45° obstruction)

- ● 500 lux at a ceiling height of 2.5 m
- ■ 50 lux at a ceiling height of 2.5 m
- ⋯ 500 lux at a ceiling height of 3 m
- ⋯ 50 lux at a ceiling height of 3 m
- × 500 lux at a ceiling height of 4 m
- ● 50 lux at a ceiling height of 4 m
- ＋ 500 lux at a ceiling height of 5 m
- ⋅ 50 lux at a ceiling height of 5 m
- — max, 2.5 m
- — max, 3 m
- — max, 4 m
- — max, 5 m

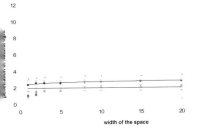

penetration of natural light, depending on the width and height of the space (60° obstruction)

- ● 500 lux at a ceiling height of 2,5 m
- ■ 50 lux at a ceiling height of 2,5 m
- ⋯ 500 lux at a ceiling height of 3 m
- ⋯ 50 lux at a ceiling height of 3 m
- × 500 lux at a ceiling height of 4 m
- ● 50 lux at a ceiling height of 4 m
- ＋ 500 lux at a ceiling height of 5 m
- ⋅ 50 lux at a ceiling height of 5 m
- — max, 2.5 m
- — max, 3 m
- — max, 4 m
- — max, 5 m

the impact of the width of a space on the depth of penetration of natural light at different angles of obstruction and ceiling heights. the street widths are 35 m, 20 m, and 12 m, respectively, for a building height of 20 m. the figures show that the differences in natural light yield level off as the external angle of obstruction increases
source: 'gevel en stad' study, delft university of technology, faculty of architecture, in cooperation with building physics and urbanism

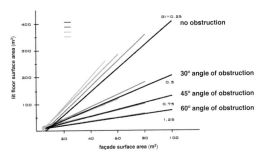

the lit floor surface area set against the façade surface area. situation with a large external angle of obstruction show that the relationship between the façade surface area and the lit floor surface area is the same in low and wide spaces as in high and narrow spaces.
only where there is no (or little) obstruction does it make a difference whether a high (and therefore narrow) or a low (and therefore wide) space.
graph based on natural light simulations at an assumed building height of 20 m.
(Fi = Façade index lit = façade surface area/lit floor surface area)

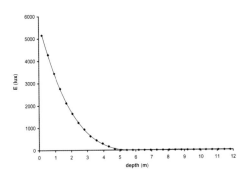

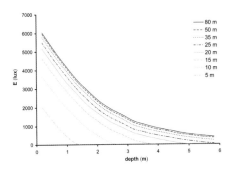

isolines of the average light intensity (in lux) in 5 different spaces, each measuring 50 m², at a façade height of 3 m. we can see that the average light intensity increases linearly with the window surface area (in other words the façade width), while the GFA remains constant. in other words, the light yield increases as the Façade index increases.
these simulations took into account reflection of natural light by the interior (reflection from walls, floors, and ceiling were respectively 50, 20 and 70 per cent)

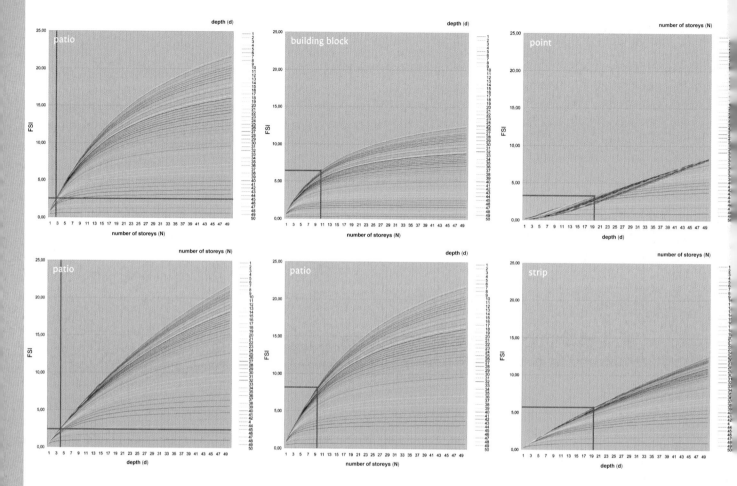

what are the minimum conditions for the fringe
depth and the number of storeys at a desired FSi
in a given building type?
the bottom graph shows that with patio building,
in order to achieve an FSi of 2.50, we have to
build a minimum of 3 storeys high and 4 m deep
(this means a fringe 2 m deep in the template)

what FSi can be attained (with a maximum
depth of 50 as a baseline point in the model)
at a set maximum building height and in a given
building type?
comparison of the maximum attainable FSi of the
patio with that of the building block, if a building
height of 30 m is allowed (10 storeys of 3 m)

what FSi can be attained at a certain depth of
the building fringe?
comparison of the maximum attainable FSi of
the point with that of the strip, if a building
height of 20 m is allowed.
with the strip, we can see that the maximum
FSi is attained by setting the number of storeys
at 50 (the maximum number storeys input in
the model).
with the point, however, we see that it is most
efficient for the FSi to build 7 storeys, instead
of the maximum number of storeys

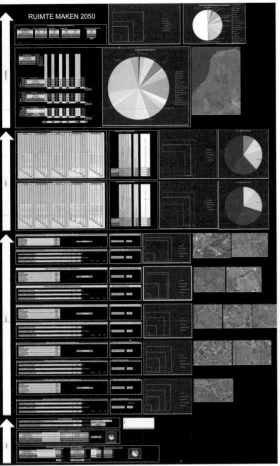

spreadsheet for the calculation of the density of the built-up area as a percentage of the netherlands with the parameters

The website www.stedenvolruimte.nl contains a number of interactive spreadsheets for density calculations. The site also provides links to related websites and is open for a forum and commentary, as well as additions to the calculation method and the book.

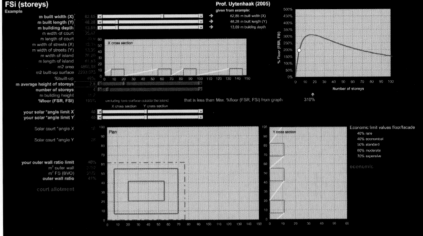

prof. taeke de jong has set up a combined spreadsheets for building blocks based on these calculations at delft university of technology, with which the calculations demonstrated here can be applied in practice.

the attained and maximum potential FSi for building block sizes input by the user are shown in the upper-right graph: run the cursor along the graph in order to vary the number of storeys, for example. natural light is still a simple function of the angle of obstruction, because the results of the natural light studies and the impact of ceiling heights on this have not yet been processed. insufficient lighting of the street\courtyard, however, is already detected, as well as the attained façade index – important for the potential of the interior in light and view and as an economic factor (see bottom right in the graph)

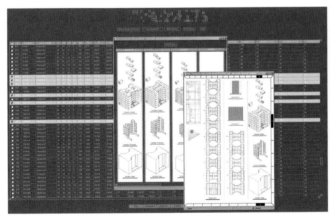

the block library (blocklib) shows 880 different building combinations between the two extreme volumes of 5×5×5 m and 50×50×50 m. values including the FSi, GSi and the Façade index are compared to one another and explicated. the 880 building configurations and the website were created by students at delft university of technology

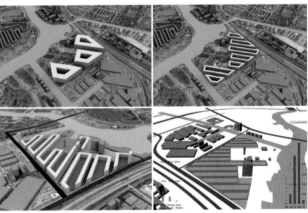

student work at delft university of technology by david spierings and remko van gijzen. different possibilities for construction at the overamstel site in amsterdam are being researched with 3-d computer models. the capacity of the proposed construction is automatically generated and displayed in interactive bar diagrams

projects discussed

typology study low rise in high density, Eindhoven
1972
plan for the Kinkerbuurt, Amsterdam
1972-1973
design Rudy Uytenhaak

building complex, Weesperstraat, Amsterdam
1980-1992
design team Rudy Uytenhaak, Felix Claus, Kees Kaan,
John Bosch *realization* Tiemen Koetsier with
Joost Hovenier, Ge van Dam

housing blocks, Czaar Peter\Conradstraat, Amsterdam
1980-2005
n40 design team Rudy Uytenhaak, Felix Claus, Kees Kaan,
John Bosch *realization* Rudy Uytenhaak, Marco Romano
n41 design team Rudy Uytenhaak, Marco Romano,
Jacobien Hofstede *realization* Andre Hillebrand,
Peter Rutten

Droogbak residential building, Amsterdam
1986-1989
design team Rudy Uytenhaak, Felix Claus *realization*
Felix Claus, Gerard Kruunenberg, Engbert van der Zaag

patio dwellings, Geuzenveld, Amsterdam
1988-1991
design team Rudy Uytenhaak, Engbert van der Zaag,
Theo Peppelman *realization* Engbert van der Zaag

Java Island study project, Amsterdam
1991
design Rudy Uytenhaak *realization* Jan Peter Wingender,
Mariette Adriaanssen, Ad van Aert, Maurits Cobben

Borneo-Sporenburg study project, Amsterdam
1993
Malaparte dwellings, Borneo Island, Amsterdam
1996-2001
design team Rudy Uytenhaak, Engbert van der Zaag,
John Zondag *realization* Engbert van der Zaag,
John Zondag, Jan Olthuis, Martin de Graaf

De Bongerd dwellings, Amsterdam-Noord
2001-2006
design team Rudy Uytenhaak, John Zondag
realization Rudy Uytenhaak architectenbureau (ao)

Olympisch Kwartier dwellings, Amsterdam-Zuid
1999-2004
design team Rudy Uytenhaak, Marco Romano with
Jos Rijs, Engbert van der Zaag, Joppe Kneppers,
Thomas Bernhardt *realization* Marco Romano with
Engbert van der Zaag, Ingrid Turpijn, Andre Hillebrand,
Tanja Buijs, Joppe Kneppers, Martin de Graaf,
Dorien Mulder, Jurgen Ditzel, Martin Dalenberg

Veltmanstraat dwellings, Amsterdam Slotervaart
1999-2003
design team Rudy Uytenhaak, Hugo Boogaard with
Chanan Hornstra, Jacobien Hofstede *realization*
Hugo Boogaard with Jan Olthuis, Martijn Pietersen

La Fenêtre residential building, The Hague
1999-2005
design team Rudy Uytenhaak, Hugo Boogaard, Jos Rijs,
Kees Stoffels *realization* Hugo Boogaard with Titia Jansen,
Jan Olthuis, Martijn Pietersen, Wouter Hilhorst

study project dwellings and dance studio, Amsterdam
2008
design study Rudy Uytenhaak

bibliography

Letty Reimerink
Grenzeloos wonen. Europa verhuist
Wormer: Inmerc 2008
isbn 978 90 6611 846 1

Huub Smeets, Rudy Uytenhaak, Han Michel
La Fenêtre
Maastricht: Vesteda architectuur 2007
isbn 90 77059 06 7

Bart Reuser, Rudy Uytenhaak 'Prototypen of reeksen'
in *De Architect*, November 2006, pp. 20-23

Rudy Uytenhaak lecture *Dynamics of density*
Delft: Delft University of Technology, Faculty of
Architecture 2005

Irene van Exel, Marije Raap (eds.) [Veltmanstraat]
*ZO, tips en trucs voor efficiënte planontwikkeling van
complexe woningbouwprojecten in Amsterdam*
Amsterdam: Ontwikkelingsbedrijf en Dienst Ruimtelijke
Ordening, Gemeente Amsterdam 2005

M. Kloos (ed.)
ARCAM pocket *Was getekend: de architect*
Amsterdam: Architectura & Natura Press 2004
isbn 90 76863 20 2

Friederike Schneider
Grundrißatlas \ Floor Plan Manual. Wohnungsbau \ Housing
Basel: Birkhäuser Verlag AG 2004
isbn 978 3 7643 6985 9

Tobias Huber 'Wohnjockey \ Studentenarbeit \ VarioFlex \
Home Mixing' in *AIT. Architektur, Innenarchitektur,
Technischer Ausbau* 2004 vol 112 no. 7\8 pp. 42-43

Irene van Exel, Eireen Schreurs (eds.) [La Fenêtre]
Wonen in de wolken. Handboek woontorens in Amsterdam
Amsterdam: Ontwikkelingsbedrijf en Dienst Ruimtelijke
Ordening Gemeente Amsterdam 2003

M.Y. Berghauser Pont, P.A. Haupt
Spacemate. The spatial logic of urban density
Delft: Delft University Press Science 2002
isbn 90 4072 530 6

P. Jansen, F. Swildens, M. Oostenbrink [Java Island]
Wonen in Compacte Amsterdamse Hoogbouw
Amsterdam: coördinatieteam Optimalisering
Grondgebruik ism Stedelijke Woningdienst
Gemeente Amsterdam 2002

Manfred Bock, Vincent van Rossem, Kees Somer
Cornelis van Eesteren, architect, urbanist [part 1]
Rotterdam: NAi Publishers \ The Hague: EFL Stichting 2001
isbn 90 7246 962 3

P. Jansen, F. Swildens, M. Oostenbrink, J. de Waal
Compact wonen [Geuzenveld-West]
Amsterdam: coördinatieteam Optimalisering
Grondgebruik, Gemeente Amsterdam 1999

MVRDV *Farmax*
Rotterdam: 010 Publishers 1999
isbn 90 6450 266 8

Woonverkenningen. Milieutypen en transformatie
The Hague: Ministry of Housing, Social Planning and
the Environment (VROM) 1997

Ton Verstegen
Rudy Uytenhaak. Architect
Rotterdam: 010 Publishers 1996
in the series of monographs on Dutch architects
isbn 90 6450 241 2

G.B. Urhahn, M. Bobic
Strategie voor stedelijkheid
Bussum: Thoth 1996
isbn 90 6868 148 6

G.B. Urhahn, M. Bobic
*A pattern image, a typological tool for quality in
urban planning*
Bussum: Thoth 1994\2000
isbn 90 6868 103 6

M. Kloos (ed.)
ARCAM pocket book *Rudy Uytenhaak. Architect*
Amsterdam: Architectura & Natura Press 1993
isbn 90 71570 30 4

Roger Sherwood
Modern Housing prototypes
Cambridge (Mass): Harvard University Press 1978
isbn 06 7457 942 9 \ isbn 978 06 7457 942 2
see also http://housingprototypes.org/bibliography

Rolf Jensen
High Density Living
London: Leonard Hill 1966
isbn 02 4938 956 8

Jaarlijkse Projectdocumentatie Gemeente Amsterdam
Amsterdam: Ontwikkelingsbedrijf Gemeente Amsterdam

Amsterdam in cijfers
Amsterdam: Stadsuitgeverij Amsterdam 2007
isbn 978 90 6274 138 0

David Keuning, 'Massa zonder zwaarte' in *De Architect*,
May 2006 p. 82 ff. (on La Fenêtre)

Rudy Uytenhaak, 'Chaos is maar onbegrepen samenhang'
in *Dax*, 2006 no. 8 pp. 4-5

Bernard Colenbrander and MUST Stedebouw (eds.)
Limes Atlas
Rotterdam: 010 Publishers 2005
isbn 90-6450-535-7

Bernard Faber, 'Berlage herleeft in Olympisch Kwartier,
Amsterdamse School opnieuw geïnterpreteerd'
in *Stedenbouw* 2004 no. 612 p. 17 ff.

Bernard Faber, 'Tussen Manhattan en Jordaan.
Uiteenlopende woonbelevingen aan de Veltmanstraat'
in *Stedenbouw*, 2003 no. 608 p. 118 ff.

Jaap Huisman 'Er is niet gauw te veel Uytenhaak'
in *Vrij Nederland*, 2002 no. 26 pp. 62-63

Janny Rodermond 'Sluitstuk lamellenstructuur Borneo'
in *De Architect*, 2002 no. 4 p. 44 ff.

Typology. Projects en studies since 1990 arranged by type
[reprinted in the back of this book]
Amsterdam: Rudy Uytenhaak architectenbureau 2000

Rudy Uytenhaak, 'Passen en meten in de stad.
Laagbouwwoningen in hogere dichtheden bouwen.
Dichtheden als een positieve kwaliteit ervaren'
interview in *Moes Inzicht*, 1995 no. 5 pp. 22-25

A. Stipa, 'Il disegno urbano nasce dalla densito di
funzioni significati e potenzialito' interview in
Controspazio, 1994 no. 2 pp. 46-63

H. Moscoviter, 'De heilige drievuldigheid van
Rudy Uytenhaak. Architectuur tussen het detail en het
grote gebaar' interview in *Items*, 1994 no. 4 pp. 18-24

M. Selie, 'De Houdini onder de architecten.
Rudy Uytenhaak' interview in *Diurna*, 1994 no. 8 p. 15

Rudy Uytenhaak, 'Een modern project met oog voor het
bestaande. De Czaar Peterbuurt moet Czaar Peterbuurt
blijven' interview in *Eigen Haard*, 1993 no. 2 pp. 3-4

I. Haagsma en H. de Haan, 'Scheve hoeken en schuine
vlakken. Architect Uytenhaak ziet het als zijn opdracht
ook de stad te verbeteren' interview in *De Volkskrant*,
6 November 1993

T. Metz, 'Verantwoordelijkheid voor de stad. Gezichts-
bepalende architectuur voor woningbouwcorporatie
Lieven de Key' in *NRC-Handelsblad*, 1993

F. den Houter, 'Plan Weesperstraat. Grachtenwoningen,
kantoren, parkeergarage' in *Stedenbouw*, 1993 no. 500
pp. 61-63

C. Hornstra, P. Vlok, 'Rudy Uytenhaak over de kwaliteit
van stedelijke dichtheid' interview in *De Omslag*, 1993
no. 11 p. 2-7

R. Morteo, 'Rudy Uytenhaak. Edificio residenziale ›De
Droogbak‹ Amsterdam' in *Domus*, 1991 no. 723 pp. 52-59

Rudy Uytenhaak, inaugural address
Ruimte dichten. Opdracht, visie en passie
Eindhoven: Eindhoven University of Technology,
Faculty of Architecture, 15 February 1991
internet: Orations THE and TU\e

H. Stoutjesdijk, 'Palazzo's in de Czaar Peterbuurt.
Uytenhaak introduceert nieuw verkavelingstype'
in *De Architect*, 1990 no. 9 pp. 100-105

G. Confurius, 'Neues aus Amsterdam. Drei Amsterdammer
architekten und ihre jüngsten Beiträge zum Sozialen
Wohnungsbau' in *Bauwelt*, 1990 no. 31 pp. 1528-1547

A. Oosterman, 'Een gebouw voor de stad. Woningbouw
van Rudy Uytenhaak in Amsterdam' in *Archis*, 1990 no. 3
pp. 36-41

Rudy Uytenhaak, 'Nieuwe Houttuinen' in *Wonen TABK* 22,
1982

Rudy Uytenhaak, 'Juiste straat en goede draad weer
opgepakt' in *Wonen TABK*, 1982 no. 18 pp. 26-43

Rudy Uytenhaak, various articles as editor of *Forum*
from 1978 to 1984, including 'Stadsvernieuwing. Vorm-
geven aan een karakteristiek' in *Forum* 28, 1984 no. 4
pp. 42-45; 'Gebouw en stad' in *Forum*, 1980 no. 2 p. 52;
book review Rowe, *Collage City* in *Forum*, 1980 no. 1;
theme issue on Bruno Taut's housing construction in
Berlin, *Forum XXVI*, 1977 no. 6

glossary

Utrecht city centre = important centre of one of the oldest cities in the Netherlands. the Oudegracht and Nieuwegracht canals flow south to north, lined with wharves, low quays onto which the wharf cellars of the canal houses open.

Les Halles, Paris = because the centre of Paris, around 1970, could no longer accommodate the growing flow of traffic, the market was relocated outside of the city, and between 1971 and 1973 the landmark market halls were demolished. now the site of a large, partially underground entertainment and shopping centre.

Kowloon City, Hong Kong = a walled village, once the domain of mafiosi, prostitution, refugees and the poor, became a small city in the 20th century: jam-packed with high-rises with as many as 20 storeys, schools on the roofs and shops on the ground floor. demolished following reunification with China in 1997. now a park.

Maupoleum, Amsterdam = the financial contribution by property dealer Maurits (Maup) Caransa for the construction of the 150-m-long Tellegenhuis on the Jodenbreestraat, earned it the nickname 'Maupoleum'. housing part of the University of Amsterdam, ridiculed from the start, it was known, during its short existence (1971-94), as the 'ugliest building in the Netherlands'.

machines for living in = 'Every home is equal, as perfect a machine à habiter as possible. Le Corbusier sought to break with an obsolete understanding of the house, a derivative of the palace and the status symbol ... to restore it to its primitive function as an instrument for living.' (Bekaert)

existenzminimum = functionalist premise of the building challenge following the First World War, which called for a home with a minimum level of comfort for everyone.

intuitive\empirical, pre-theoretical mechanics = rope bridges and aqueducts. Roman aqueducts attained a standard of engineering that would not be equalled for 1,000 years. several are still in use in North Africa.

'Goois' or 'Wassenaars' living ideal = Het Gooi, an area of rolling hills east of Amsterdam with important protected nature areas, authentic villages and villa developments. Wassenaar, near The Hague, is a village core in a wooded setting with numerous villas and mansions (many of them originally country houses for rich city-dwellers). in many places, recently built pastiches of this form a 'suburban hybrid, neither fish nor fowl'.

housing density = the number of dwellings per hectare (in Anglo-Saxon culture, inhabitants per hectare).

FSi, Floor Space index = objectively represents how efficient the use of space is. in numerical terms, equivalent to building percentage × stacking factor.

tare telescope = instrument to visualize urban design profiles. shows the proportion of net to gross surface area at various levels of scale and makes it possible to compare urban tissues.

societal, political = making density measurable provides an instrument to monitor developments, describe option scenarios clearly and implement them when opinions have been formed and decisions taken.

topographic = red (built), green (unbuilt), blue (water), white (infrastructure). when we blow up the topographic map to the scale of the city map, we see that 'red' is made up of green, blue and white spaces, surrounded by a red urban mass.

Nolli = the 'new map of Rome' (1748) by engineer Giovanni Battista Nolli includes the interior of public buildings in the space of streets and squares.

CIAM district = developed according to urban-design insights of the *Congrès Internationaux d'Architecture Moderne* starting in 1928, with the segregation of functions as the main characteristic of large-scale urban expansions. after 1959 (Team 10), new insights eventually led to the rehabilitation of the city itself: urban renewal.

Westelijke Tuinsteden, Amsterdam = 'Western Garden Suburbs', an expansion district in the west of Amsterdam built in the 1950s and 1960s.

the more exact subject of this book = the moment when 'the red' of the flat, 2-D urban design of the planning map turns into 3-D models. where drawings become polystyrene foam models. focus is on the interaction of the mass & space it contains with the adjustment of this material. goal: a density of meaning and spatial quality.

the 'park city' of thinkers such as Walter Gropius and Le Corbusier is based on the absolutization of stacking. 'light and air' were understood within too simple a parameter (as the angle of obstruction to light penetration on the façade). high slabs and towers in empty fields seldom produce interesting areas.

the TU spreadsheet shows what densities can be achieved with 4 building types (point, patio, strip, block building).

façade index = the ratio between the façade surface and the gross floor surface area. the façade quantity determines the building costs to a large extent, but in addition, the more façade a building has, the better the light penetration, the more generous the view and the more impressive the sense of space.

the departments of Housing, Building Physics and Urbanism at Delft University of Technology are conducting research in order to arrive at more rational considerations in the production of new urban volumes, using light-engineering performance. the knowledge acquired makes it possible to refine the existing, somewhat simplistic rules of thumb.

the Permeta 'Spacemate' provides a systematic approach to density at the urban design level.

the building percentage, stacking factor and angle of obstruction primarily determine the density.

toposphere = man builds and lives where the *troposphere* and the *lithosphere* intertwine: from mines and cellars to penthouses and office buildings. folds and hollows in the toposphere maximize the contact surface for interaction. this porous layer reaches its maximum thickness in the layeredness of most urban areas: from the top of towers to the bottom of cellars, tunnels, cable conduits.

standard dwelling = in the Netherlands, 100 years of housing legislation has resulted in a far-reaching rationalization of the standard reference dwelling. the floor space of the reference home grew from about 60 m^2 in 1960 to 80 m^2 in 1980 to the present 95 m^2.

Roger Sherwood argued in 1978 that the home is organized according to its orientation and the residential building according to its access.

the *blocklib* programme provides a new palette of meaningful hybrid residential buildings that cannot be categorized as one standard type or the other.

back-to-back patio types on Borneo Island = peninsula in the Eastern Harbour District of Amsterdam.

superblocks on Java Island = peninsula in the Eastern Harbour District of Amsterdam.

towers on the Müllerpier = spit on the west side of Rotterdam city centre.

patio blocks on the Funen = triangle bordering the Czaar Peterbuurt, east of Amsterdam city centre.

density cannot come at the expense of enjoyment of the home = the dwelling, residential building and surrounding public space must provide *compensation for the density achieved* through natural light penetration, access, views, privacy and the quality of the (semi-) public space.

proximity increases the opportunities for communication, commerce, cooperation, influence.

Maslow's Hierarchy of Needs = 1. organic, physical; 2. safety & security, 3. social contact, 4. esteem & recognition and 5. self-actualization (\transcendence).

densely built cities take up less space, land, and infrastructure (roads, pipes, cables, lighting, etc) and require less maintenance. they do consume distance, privacy.

the architect mediates between the city and intimacy. makes neither, perhaps the space in between. see also Rudy Uytenhaak's inaugural address, 1991 (bibliography).

orientation is an element of the perception of the space. a city that is too easily memorable and legible is dull. those who proceed through the city are guided by continuity and variation, certainly when the same route is travelled often. a balance between legibility & variation, reassurance & stimulation, order & surprise.

Ildefons Cerdà (1815-1876) = architect of the grid of octagonal blocks of the Eixample (Ensanche) in Barcelona – which in the early 19th century had the highest housing density in Europe. famed example of scientific urbanism (1859) provided for housing for the wealthy middle class, small independent merchants, as well as workers.

the Passeig de Gràcia in Barcelona = exclusive shopping street, 3 km long, that runs across the Eixample.

Camillo Sitte (1843-1903) = architect, urban design theorist, of great significance to the development of planning, urbanism and urban regulation in Europe.

Novartis Quarter in Basel = chemical giant (Ciba+Geigy+Sandoz) is transforming its industrial site on the Rhine into a knowledge centre, based on a master plan by Vittorio Lampugnani (ETH Zürich). an elite group of architects have been building there since 2006.

H.P. Berlage (1856-1934) = influential architect and urban designer: Amsterdam-Zuid expansion plan. Berlage created combinations of closed housing blocks (Plan Zuid, from 1904 onward).

Cornelis van Eesteren (1897-1988) = architect and urban designer. involved in CIAM. head of the Urban Development Section of the Amsterdam Public Works Department from 1929 to 1959. designed, with Th. van Lohuizen, the Amsterdam General Expansion Plan of 1934-35, the basis for urban expansions in the 1950s and 1960s. spiritual father of the functional city, with strictly segregated functions of housing, work, traffic, recreation and nature. his finger-city model, with urban lobes and green wedges, can be identified in Amsterdam. Van Eesteren made templates of high-rise buildings: 'fields' (Buitenveldert, from 1958 onward).

flaneur = urbanite, described according to the Parisian life of the boulevards: the flâneur lets himself be seen and in the meantime observes, slightly indifferent. (*Passagenwerk*, Walter Benjamin).

an architecture of encounter and interweaving is central to Le Corbusier's and also to Herman Hertzberger's work: the commune-residential building replaces the street.

Hoop, Liefde en Fortuin = residential building in Amsterdam on the Rietlandpark (Eastern Harbour District) parallel to the entrance of the Piet Hein Tunnel. the inclined north façade links 202 rental and 167 owner-occupied flats and facilities. elderly residents are combined with relatively large families and starting residents. only the outside portal is communal, for the rest, individual staircases: to reduce the probability of unwelcome encounters and mutual irritations as much as possible, the semi-public route has been kept short.

the Justus van Effencomplex (Rotterdam Spangen, 1922) by Michiel Brinkman features a broad gallery with multiple access: residents can go left or right. this principle of multiple entrances is seldom applied.

Frans van Gool uses each of his galleries in Amsterdam-Noord (Buikslotermeer, 1966-70) to provide access to three storeys at a time. you use stairs to go up or down: here the corridor access has been modified.

the corridor as a narrow, oppressive hallway in the heart of the building is reminiscent of a hotel or nursing home: shifting the corridor to the façade at least takes care of the initial objection.

Alison en Peter Smithson shifted, as it were, the corridor of their Golden Lane residential building (London, 1953), which provided access to several storeys, to the façade.

Liesbeth van der Pol combined back-to-back and zigzag housing, so that each dwelling has two different views (Twiske-West 1993 and GWL-site 1994, Amsterdam)

the ideal view is multifaceted and layered. not just over the city but actually over the network, the 'breeding ground'. view of highly diverse urban spheres: river, park, square, garden, sky.

Ettore Scola's film 'Una giornata particolare' (1977) was shot in and on the collective roof terrace of a high-rise on the Viale XXI Aprile in Rome, built during the boom of Fascist building activity in the 1930s.

in Hans Scharoun's Siemensstadt (1929-31) the storage areas, including the deck chairs, are located on the collective roof terrace.

view linked to spaciousness = in Gerrit Rietveld's Schröder House (1924) you walk upstairs looking at a blank wall; only when you turn can you see outside through the large corner window: the contrast reinforces the effect. a comparable effect was achieved in the dwellings on Borneo Island. upstairs, first the virtually blank front façade, then turn a quarter turn and look out through a large sliding glass window in the side wall, through a terrace, over the water. it brings the outside in.

building regulations = Building Decree (national government) and Building Ordinances (municipalities).

cluttered landscape = unbridled construction of commercial estates and new housing development in hitherto undisturbed areas of the Dutch landscape.

9 measures = that could simplify and stimulate research into and the design of attractive, spacious, densely built cities.

laws of density = mathematical research into the rules upon which the built environment is based.

credits

publication commemorating the completion of Rudy Uytenhaak's professorship in architecture related to practice at Delft University of Technology, Faculty of Architecture, Chair of Dwelling

with research and contributions by
Jeroen Mensink, Bart Reuser, Marijn Schenk, Saskia Oranje, Renske Appel, Simon de Ruijter, Peter Mensinga
with gratitude to
Meta Berghauser Pont and Per Haupt,
Truus de Bruijn-Hordijk and Marjolein van Esch,
Taeke de Jong

this publication was made possible by
Delft University of Technology, Faculty of Architecture
de Alliantie Ontwikkeling, Huizen
AM Wonen BV, Nieuwegein
Amvest Vastgoed BV, Amsterdam Zuid-Oost
Dienst Stedenbouw en Volkshuisvesting, Rotterdam
Ontwikkelingsbedrijf Gemeente Amsterdam
De Key\Principaal, Amsterdam
NS Vastgoed, Utrecht
Rabo Bouwfonds, Haarlem
Vesteda Groep BV, Maastricht
Ministerie van Volkshuisvesting, Ruimtelijke Ordening en Milieu,
Directie Nationale Ruimtelijke Ordening
Dienst RO\EZ, Gemeente Groningen
Rudy Uytenhaak Architectenbureau, Amsterdam

illustrations in cooperation with
Berte Daan, Saskia Oranje, Duco Uytenhaak
3d animations David Spierings, Remko van Gijzen
cover illustration Bouke Veurman, Erik van de Hart, TU Delft Architecture
photography of projects Pieter Kers, Luuk Kramer, Theo Uytenhaak (ao)

text Rudy Uytenhaak
editor Jeroen Mensink
final editor Ed Melet
English translation InOtherWords, Pierre Bouvier
English copy editor D'Laine Camp
graphic design Jaap van Triest

printed by Die Keure, Brugge

© 2008 010 Publishers, Rotterdam
www.010.nl

isbn 978-90-6450-674-1 [english edition]
isbn 978-90-6450-669-7 [dutch edition]

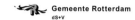